DON'T BE AFRAID

A German War Bride Becomes an American

Bardolf & Company

DON'T BE AFRAID: A German War Bride Becomes an American

ISBN 978-1938842-46-7
Copyright © 2020 by Waltraut Stanton

Published by Bardolf & Company
www.bardolfandcompany.com

Cover design by Shaw Creative
www.shawcreativegroup.com

To my parents,
Erwin and Rosa Kleiber

Everywhere immigrants have strengthened and enriched the fabric of American life.

—John. F. Kennedy

DON'T BE AFRAID

A German War Bride Becomes an American

Wally Stanton

Bardolf & Company
Sarasota, Florida

Contents

Introduction

I owe everything to my parents, Erwin and Rosa Kleiber.

My mother was the most courageous woman I have ever known. During and after World War II, she took care of my brother and me on her own. She was tough, yet never angry; never complained about spending exhausting days going into the Berlin countryside to barter for food. She simply did what was necessary. I've tried to put myself in her place many times and ask, "Could I have done what she did?" I'd like to think I would have.

My father was a loving parent, too, both before and after the war. He never complained either, even though serving in the German army and being imprisoned in Russia damaged his health. He did his best to restore our family life to normal and urged me to make the best of my opportunities.

Both my parents instilled in me a can-do spirit which I discovered, when I came to the Unites States, is also a fine American trait. By example and encouragement, they taught me to keep going in adversity, overcome fear, take risks, and enjoy life to the fullest. Although they were sad to see me emigrate to the United States, they never tried to hold me back, never stood in the way of me seeking a better life.

Coming to this country wasn't easy, however. Except for my husband, Owen, I knew no one here, and it took a while for me to get settled. Most people I met were kind, generous and welcoming, displaying another fine American trait that make this country so special—a big heart.

Many, when they found out I'd grown up in Germany, asked me about my experiences. My first husband's relatives wanted to know what it had been like there during and after the war. My children did, too. As they grew up, I'd tell them stories about Berlin, their relatives, and how I survived, and they pressed me for more. Many times, people told me, "You should write a book."

My daughter Shirley and granddaughter Diana urged me to do so, too, and the idea slowly grew on me. After moving to the West Coast of Florida, I decided the time was right to write about my life. My son David encouraged me in the undertaking as well. I cannot thank them enough. I could not have done it without their support.

I also wish to thank Chris Angermann, without whose help I would not have been able to tell my story fully. His guiding me through the process of bringing this book to publication has been a blessing.

There is another reason I wanted to write *Don't Be Afraid*, besides sharing my memories and experiences. After I arrived in New York and settled in Huntington, Long Island, not everyone welcomed me with open arms. Some people, when they found out where I came from said, "Oh, you're German—you're a Nazi." Several schoolmates of my daughter called her that derogatory name, too.

I know that such offensive behavior comes mostly from ignorance, but plenty of prejudiced people parade their views that way, putting others down to make themselves feel better. I have come to realize that they are frightened, unhappy human beings, and it is best to pay no attention to them.

But I do want to set the record straight. As a young girl growing up in Nazi Germany, I had no idea what ghastly, murderous policies the Hitler regime pursued. Even if I had, there was nothing I could have done about it. The same was true for many other Germans who did not support Hitler but kept quiet to survive.

In wartime, civilians everywhere go through hardships not of their own making and suffer the consequences of the decisions made by political and military leaders. That was the case in Germany, too. While no one in my immediate family was subjected to the horrors of concentration camps or Hitler's brutal genocide, we also suffered. Many a night, we endured horrific air raids, cowering in the basement while bombs rained down on our city. We often went to bed hungry. We lost relatives dear to us.

In retrospect, I believe we should look kindly on those who were powerless in the face of brute aggression, recognize their humanness, and treat them with tolerance and respect.

We are fortunate to have a country that cherishes freedom and diversity and gives us the right to pursue happiness, each in our own way. I have lived here now for more than sixty years, proud of my heritage, and proud of my home. I always say, "I once was a German, but I am an American now!"

Wally Stanton
Venice, Florida 2020

1
Wedding District

I was born in Berlin, Germany, on March 10, 1934, in the Paul-Gerhardt-Stift, a Protestant hospital, about a mile from my parents' apartment building. We lived in the Wedding District of Berlin about two miles northwest of the city's center, where all the famous tourist spots are located—the Alexanderplatz, museums and theaters, and the Brandenburg Gate. The area was considered a tough, working-class neighborhood by some, but that was not my experience growing up. I played outside on the street, walked to and from school three-quarters of a mile away, and did errands for my parents without ever worrying about my safety.

We lived on the second floor of a corner apartment building where two streets met in a sharp bend. There were only four tall buildings on the one-block Weddingstrasse (Wedding Street), with house numbers 2 to 5. Ours was number 2. If you turned left to go up Kösliner Strasse, which was a single block street, too, but three times as long, you passed a delicatessen/grocery store and another way into our building. The entrances led to separate ground floor lobbies and apartments on the three floors above. On our side, a wooden staircase with a curved banister ran along the wall to a landing and then up to a mezzanine overlooking the entrance foyer. From there, it was just a few steps to our apartment.

On the corner of the intersection stood a *Litfasssäule*, a concrete column the size of a small kiosk, plastered with announcements and advertisements. Farther down, on the Kösliner Strasse were a tobacco store and a butcher shop on our side, and a tavern, a hair salon, and a coal dealer across the street.

My earliest memory is of my brother being born in our apartment when I had just turned two. My mother had put me in my crib next to the window and was walking back and forth, holding her belly. From time to time, she would say to me, "Lie down," and put a blanket over me. But I always pulled it off and popped up to see what she was doing. It made her mad, but she kept walking. Sometimes, she stopped and clenched a fist and scrunched up her face in pain. At some point, my grandmother Minna arrived and told her to lie down on the bed. Soon my mother started to scream. Then she stopped for a while before screaming again. That happened a number of times. It sounded so loud and agonizing, I squeezed my eyes shut and put my hands over my ears.

Later, I learned that everything had gone well, and my brother had been born in the bed. But then my mother started to bleed. My grandmother hurried to the deli downstairs where there was a telephone. She called an ambulance to take her and my brother to the hospital. While they and my father, who had rushed home from work, were gone, my grandmother took me to the cottage in a wooded park where she and my grandfather lived. When I returned home some days later, my mother and brother were back in the apartment from the hospital, and everything was fine.

My parents named him Horst Kurt Otto.

I had only one name, Waltraut, although when I was a young girl, everybody called me Trauty. My father was very affectionate and loving. He called me *Murkel*—shrimp—and would take me on his lap

14

and rock me back and forth. When I asked him why I had only one name, he said he had read it in a book about the *Nibelungenlied*, the German national epic. It belonged to one of the Valkyries, the warrior women who rode into battle on winged horses and carried the fallen heroes to Valhalla, the home of the gods. It meant "strong, powerful ruler," and he'd figured that was all the name I needed.

I still have the document from my christening. My mother's oldest brother, Uncle Reinhart and his wife, Aunt Ellie, stood as my godparents. For a present, she gave me a set of coral and gold earrings. As I got older, I couldn't wait until my mother pierced my ears so I could wear them. I slept with them and never took them off. They were part of me.

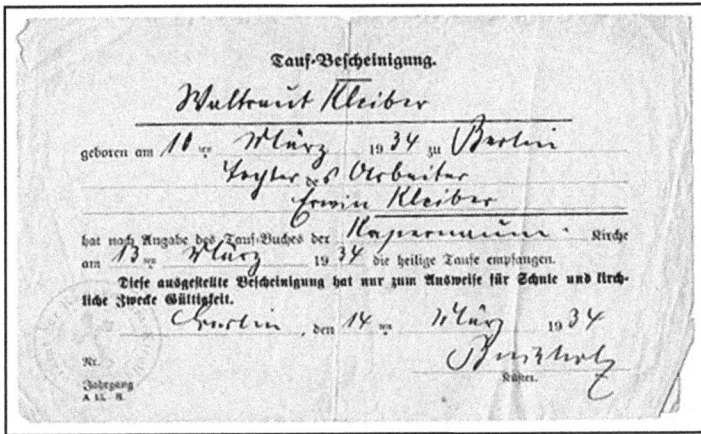

My baptism certificate.

Our apartment wasn't very big. My brother and I slept in the small side room. My parents had their bed in the corner of the living room. During the day, it became a kind of couch and served as a sitting area. In the kitchen stood a big, coal-burning stove with white tiles on the side. The burners on top had several black, iron rings. If my mother needed a hotter fire, she'd take some of the rings out with a metal tong so that the flames heated the pots and kettle directly.

On Saturdays, my mother would heat water in a big pot and pour it into a tub set on two kitchen chairs. Then, my brother and I would climb in one at a time and take a bath. My mother would wash us with soap that came in hard, amber-colored cakes. We'd take turns from week to week as to who went first. I hated to go after Horst because, by then, the water was gray and soapy and barely lukewarm.

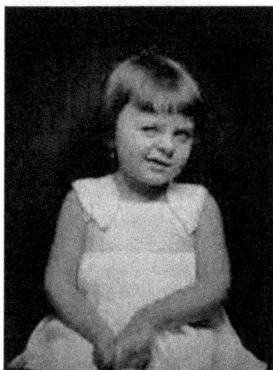

Me at age two.

My mother also did laundry once a month. She would wash underwear separately in the kitchen and hang it up in the bathroom to dry over the sink and toilet. We took the rest of the clothes and linens to the attic above the fourth floor of the building. It was a large, open room with the rafters of the flat roof exposed. There was an oven for heating water in a big copper basin, in which she cleaned shirts, dish towels, and bedsheets using a washboard. My mother had to stoke the fire really well to make the water hot enough to get all the stains out. She would scrub each item, wring it out by hand, and hang it on the laundry lines that were strung across the attic.

We carried the wet bedsheets in a big wicker basket downstairs and across the street to a store that sold cleaning goods—soap, washtubs, brooms, mops, and dust rags. The owner let us use her big roller press in back. My mother would fold the linens the way she wanted them and run them through the large wringer. They came out on the other side with no wrinkles and dry enough to store in our cupboard upstairs.

We paid a reduced monthly rent because my mother also took care of the upkeep of the apartment building, daily sweeping the stairs and foyer, and washing the sidewalk in front of the entrance. Once a week, she dragged the metal garbage cans to the curb for pickup. She was a busy, hard-working woman.

My father worked in the shipping department of Siemens, one of the largest manufacturing companies in Germany, that made light bulbs, electrics trains, radios and dynamos for electrical works. The Berlin facilities were so big that they occupied their own district, Siemensstadt (Siemens City), about three miles due east from where we lived. In the morning, my father would ride his black BMW motorcycle there wearing knickers and knee socks.

On weekends, he liked to take trips into the countryside and forests surrounding Berlin. The motorcycle had a sidecar, large enough for my brother and me to fit inside next to each other. My mother would sit on the bike behind my father with her arms around him, and he'd take off. We couldn't look outside because the wind was too strong and we didn't have goggles. If it started to rain, my father would stop and put a cover over us, and we'd lie in the dark in the sidecar. The first few times, the bumpy ride made our backs ache, but then my mother sewed special pillows for us that absorbed the shocks of the cobblestone and dirt roads.

At Siemens, my father's job was to build wooden crates for the large pieces of machinery that the company sent all over Germany and to other countries. He was good with his hands and could make just about anything. We never had to go to a shoemaker. My father owned a three-legged, metal cobbler's bench, which he stored in the basement of our building. If we needed new soles or heels for our shoes, he would nail them on himself.

The owners of the deli downstairs, Mr. and Mrs. Sawada, were generous, salt-of-the-earth people. Their relatives in the country owned a farm and sent them carrots, onions, potatoes, peas, celery, cabbage, and other vegetables to sell in their store. They had flour, cheese, and other dairy products, too. I still remember the chunks of yellow butter floating in a metal tray filled with water, sitting on a shelf in back of the glass counter.

The Sawadas son, Kurt, was my age. He, my brother, and I often spent time together in our apartment. Kurt would bring small bags of oatmeal, cocoa powder, and sugar upstairs, and we'd play "store," divvying them up and "selling" them to each other. Sometimes, we'd stir all the ingredients together, huddle under the dining table, and eat them. The concoction was dry and tasted odd. When we tried to talk, it made us cough, and a brown cloud would billow from our mouths.

One Christmas, after watching us play, my father decided to surprise me with an unexpected present. On Christmas Eve, my mother washed us in the tub and dressed us in our best clothes while my father decorated the tree in the living room. We had to wait in the kitchen until he was ready. Then, my mother let us in to see the Tannenbaum covered with tinsel, shiny ornaments, and real, red wax candles that flickering brightly and had a shimmering, mystical glow. We stared with eyes big as saucers until there was a knock at the front door.

My father called out, "Okay, Santa Claus, come in and put the presents for Trauty and Horst under the tree."

The man who came in wore a red outfit and white beard and had a hemp bag slung over his shoulder. I could tell it was Mr. Sawada from downstairs beneath the disguise—it was always him, every year—but it didn't diminish the magic of the moment. He put his sack down and asked, "Were you good children this year?" When we nodded eagerly, he opened the bag and pulled out our presents.

That year, there was a big box for me. When I tore away the wrapping paper, I was amazed to find a small wooden cabinet with shelves, bins, and drawers that pulled out. My father had constructed a little storage cupboard. There was a small scale, too. It made our playing "store" much more fun, measuring out the dry goods and wrapping them in small paper bags my mother folded for us—they looked like dark brown ice cream cones.

Another year, I asked for a doll house. That Christmas, Santa was already in the living room when we came in from the kitchen. Next to him on the floor by the tree stood a beautiful little house with a gabled roof. The rooms inside were filled with miniature furniture. My mother had upholstered the chairs and sofa and sown curtains for the windows. In back of the kitchen wall, behind the sink, my father had hooked up a small tank. When I turned the on faucet, there was running water!

The following year, my brother wanted a castle. So, my father built one with a moat, towers, and ramparts. He poured molten lead and tin into forms to make soldiers and knights. When they cooled down and hardened, he painted them so they looked like they were wearing Prussian army uniforms and medieval armor. They were so beautiful and shiny.

My parents had the ability to make something out of nothing.

Although we kids played indoors a lot, we also spent time on the street. In the winter, we had snowball fights. When the weather got warmer, we'd play kickball with the other children in the neighborhood. Usually, it was boys against girls, which meant my team always lost, but we didn't mind. During spring and summer showers, the rain often came down on only one side of the street, and we'd switch our games to whatever sidewalk remained dry. In the summer, it didn't get dark until late, and we'd play until supper time, which was around 8 p.m..

On weekend evenings, my mother's brothers—Uncle Helmut, Herbert, Kurt, and Reinhardt—would come to our apartment to play Skat. Unlike American card games, Skat has only 32 cards, although it has four suits. Since it is a game for only three players, they'd deal out three hands and take turns playing. At the end of the night, they'd tally the scores to determine the overall winner.

Uncle Reinhardt was the oldest. Although he had a factory job, he was fussy and finicky and always dressed like a gentleman. He wore shirts with starched collars, and his dark hair was parted in the middle, just so. Uncle Herbert worked at a coal store. He smelled of soot and coal dust, and the tips of his fingernails were pitch black. I liked Uncle Helmut, who seemed carefree and liked to smile. But my favorite was Uncle Kurt, who always had a good word for me when he came to our apartment. He was the youngest of the four brothers and quite handsome, although not as handsome as my father.

My brother and I watched as they played cards, drank beer, smoked cigarettes and told jokes and stories. We had a large glass slipper with a gold heel that they used as a beer pitcher, and they would pour from it to fill their glasses. When it became empty, it gurgled. Whoever was replenishing his glass at the time had to pay for the next round. He'd give me money and sent me downstairs to the tavern across the street for a refill. The place was heavy with smoke, too, and smelled musty and sour from spilled beer. A radio blared in the background, and the patrons, mostly working men from the neighborhood, were loud and boisterous, having a good time. I'd go up to the bar, put the coins on the counter, and the bartender would fill the slipper to the brim from the tap. Then, I'd walk back to our apartment, careful not to spill anything. I liked the smell of the fresh beer much better than the inside of the bar.

In retrospect, I'm surprised that my father and uncles would entrust me with such an important job. Maybe, they were engrossed in their card games and didn't want to take the time to do it themselves. Although I was thin as a rail and tall for my age, I was well-coordinated. In any case, I liked getting beer for them. It made me feel important.

Some weekends, we visited my mother's parents, Kurt and Johanna, who lived in a small, two-room apartment in the Moabit district, north of the Berlin Zoo. Their street, Sickingenstrasse, had three apartment houses with small courtyards between them. They lived in the last one on the top floor. Beyond their building ran railroad tracks. In between was a cabbage field whose owners used human manure as fertilizer, and it stank up the whole neighborhood. On warm days, you had to hold your nose as you got closer and dash into the house as fast as possible. My grandparents kept the apartment windows shut to prevent the stench from coming inside.

My grandparents, Kurt and Johanna Merten.

They were an odd couple. My grandfather was what people called "*ein alter Preusse*—an old Prussian," conservative and authoritarian. His clothes were always perfect, the crease in his pants razor-sharp, and he wore shiny, leather shoes that covered his ankles. He came from a wealthy family and had grown up on a large estate in Eberswalde, thirty miles north of Berlin, where he'd had a nursemaid and a nanny who dressed him in the mornings and took care of him all day. When he was a young man, he met my grandmother, who was a milkmaid, and they fell in love. When he insisted on marrying her, his parents disowned him.

But he remained on good terms with his younger brother, Kuno, who became a banker. Still, with us children, he always seemed a bit distant—formal and stiff. He never let me sit on his lap. Yet, when I was born, he was so proud that while my parents cleaned the apartment, he would come over, take me in the carriage, and parade me all over the neighborhood.

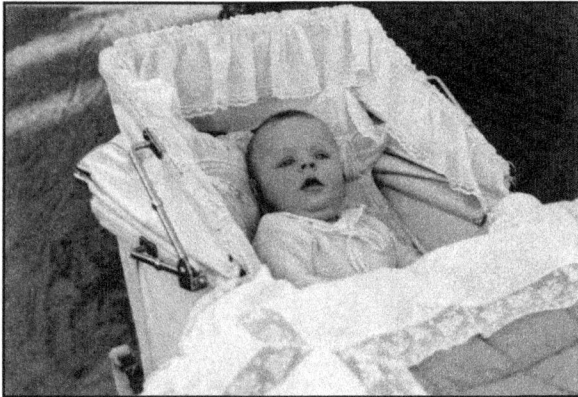

Me as a baby in my stroller.

My grandfather had worked for the railroad. By the time I knew him, he was already retired. He always sat by the kitchen window, smoking a pipe and taking it easy. Meanwhile, my grandmother was on her hands and knees, scrubbing the kitchen floor, cooking, and cleaning. She was a short woman and wore her gray hair in a bun. She had a sunny disposition and was always smiling. I could understand why my grandfather had fallen in love with her.

I still remember watching with awe as she took a hunk of rye bread, held it close to her chest, and cut all around the outside with a knife, carving it into thick pieces. Then, she'd spread lard on them as a treat for us. It was delicious. I never grew tired of watching her perform this impressive feat at family get-togethers (I didn't encounter sliced bread until came to America). As some of my baby cousins got older, when she took out her knife to carve up a loaf of bread, they lined up in the kitchen to watch her, too.

In contrast, my father's parents, Otto and Wilhelmina (the female version of William) were both friendly and outgoing. My grandfather was always joking around. We children had to shake his hand when we met him, and he'd curl up one of his fingers, trying to make us believe he'd lost it. Oma Minna, who had come to help when Horst was born, was his second wife. They lived in a cottage in a wooded park on the Schiller Heights, not too far away from us. It was part of a large colony of 250 or so summer homes. The whole area belonged to Siemens, and you could live there only

My grandfather, Otto Kleiber, and his second wife, Minna.

if you were a current or former employee of the company. My grandfather had winterized the place so they could live there year-round. Oma was still a farm girl at heart, and she grew vegetables and kept goats and sheep.

My parents owned a cottage there, too, directly across a dirt path from my grandfather. We would go there on weekends when the weather got warmer in late April, early May, and spend the whole summer season there. My father would join us after work.

There were only two other houses in our section of the heights. One belonged to a Polish couple, the Parlows. They spoke German with a strong accent and were very nice to us children. The other couple that lived there had a beautiful apple tree in the backyard. Some of the branches reached over to our side of the fence, and we'd pluck the ripe apples and eat then. We had a plum tree ourselves. In early fall, my mother would make a torte with the purple prune plums and cinnamon. It was delicious.

At my grandfather's garden house—Oma Minna and her son from her first marriage, holding me.

When my father bought our cottage, it was in run-down condition. He fixed it up, installing a modern kitchen with running water and electricity, and enclosing the porch with windows he obtained from Siemens. That's where my brother and I slept. We each had a bed and a drawer in a small dresser for our clothes. We even had a shower—a real treat in the hot, humid summer weather when we lived there full-time. My mother tended a small vegetable garden.

When we were little, my father built a sandbox for my brother and me to play in. He also set aside a small area for each of us to have our own little garden. Horst and I grew carrots and radishes. When they were ripe, we'd pull them out, clean them off, and eat them right then and there. Fresh out of the ground, they tasted sweet.

My father also raised rabbits at the cottage. He built a hutch for them with cages on three levels. Most of the females were pregnant, so we always had little ones coming. They had no hair when they were born, just reddish skin, and they didn't look very pretty. Even when they became fuzzy and cute bunnies, we didn't give them names because we knew we'd be eating them. My grandmother would do the killing for us, and we'd have rabbit for supper. I didn't like the taste—I wouldn't eat it today—but it provided us with extra meat at the time. During the winter months, we kept the rabbits the basement of our apartment building, next to the bins where we stored our coal.

At the other end of the park from our cottage was a small grocery store on the grounds where we could by drinks and watermelons. We also purchased *Schnittsalat* in boxes, leafy lettuce you could keep cutting and it would continue to grow. I helped my mother prepare dinner. We'd have salad and vegetables from the garden—green beans and white cabbage.

We spend most of the time outdoors, except when it rained. Then we would sit inside and listen to the drops pelting the windows and roof. Sometimes, thunderstorms blew across the city. My father would count the seconds between the lightning strikes and thunderclaps to determine how far away the storm was. Every three seconds meant one kilometer, and we were always happy when it passed by in the distance and didn't roar directly overhead.

At the end of the summer, when it was time to go back home, there was a big *Kinderfest*, a carnival for children, on the meadow near the entrance with carousel rides, swings, game booths and all kinds of food, candy, and toys. As it got dark, each of us children got a stick of wood with a candle on top and a paper collar to protect our hands from the wax drippings. It was like a mini-torch and when lit, the flickering light would shine through the paper. In the evenings, a band played polkas and waltzes, and the adults would dance on a wooden floor laid over a section of the meadow. It was a fun way to celebrate the end of the season, although I was always sad to leave.

Except for our stay at the summer park, during the time before I went to *Volksschule*—elementary school—my world consisted of the corner of the intersection of Weddingstrasse and Kösliner Strasse. I was too young to be aware of politics and the Nazi regime. We didn't have a radio, and until first grade, I never had to give the Hitler salute. If there were parades in Berlin, which was the seat of the government, my parents never took us. At family get-togethers, there was no discussion about what was going on in the world.

In retrospect, I suppose, the silence was telling. Neither my parents nor my aunts and uncles or grandparents were followers of Hitler or members of the Nazi party. My grandfather's second wife had a son from her previous marriage, Werner, who became an SS paratrooper, but I didn't find that out until later.

To say I had an idyllic childhood would be an understatement. It may have been sheltered and protected, but I felt safe, cherished, and loved by my parents.

The first cloud on the horizon appeared in March of 1939. I remember it so well because it happened on the weekend of my fifth birthday. Spring came early that year, and it was warm enough to visit our garden cottage for the first time. We packed food and bags and walked to the Schiller Heights. Although there were still patches of snow everywhere, crocus and other spring flowers were peeking through the dark brown earth. When we got to our cottage, it smelled stale and musty inside, and my parents threw open all the windows to air it out.

Later that weekend, I overheard a conversation between my parents and our neighbors about how things were getting bad in Poland and Russia. At some point, Mrs. Parlow said, "We're going to be in a war," and everyone stopped talking for a while.

Later, I asked my father, "What is a war?"

He said, "It's when one country fights with another country."

"Mrs. Parlow said that we're going to be in a war," I replied. "How does she know that?"

He thought for a moment. "She doesn't really know it, but she feels it," he said. "She has a hunch."

Although I didn't understand what he meant, I pretended I was satisfied with his answer. Before long, I didn't think about it anymore, and we spent another pleasant summer at our garden cottage.

But that September, shortly after we returned to our apartment for good, Germany invaded Poland and everything changed.

Horst, my mother, and I.

2

Early War Years

Suddenly, everybody talked about the war, although I still didn't understand what it meant. People seemed pleased how quickly the German armies and our Russian allies gobbled up Poland. Everyone wondered what France and England would do. Both had declared war two days after the invasion, but weeks went by, then months, and nothing happened. Later, that period would become known as the Phony War.

Fighting in the west didn't start until the following spring around the time of my sixth birthday. Words I never heard before filled the air, like Panzer, Siegfried Line, and Blitzkrieg. News about the German army's overwhelming victories in Belgium and France was on everyone's lips. But nothing changed in our day-to-day lives.

What mattered to my family was that my father got sick. He started to have fever attacks, during which he broke out in sweats and shook with chills. Sometimes, he felt so weak he couldn't go to work for several days. When the fits passed, he felt normal for a while, but then they returned and the cycle started all over again. At first, his doctors were baffled. Finally, one of them came up with a diagnosis—malaria! Some of the wood he used to build the shipping crates at Siemens had come from Africa embedded with mosquitoes that survived the journey. One of them must have bitten my father, infecting him with the tropical disease. The doctors had never seen such a case before, which why it took them so long to figure it out. For eleven months, my father was in an out of the hospital. At times, he had extended stays to receive treatments.

To make matters worse, my brother Horst also had to cope with a difficult medical condition. He had been born with crooked legs and had difficulty walking. When my mother took him to the doctors, they put his lower legs in a cast to straighten them, first one, then the other, then both at the same time. My mother had her hands full caring for him and carrying him around. He couldn't move about on his own or play with me and had to lie in bed. Eventually, the doctors took the casts off, and he could walk much better, but one leg remained a little crooked. He didn't have a limp, but I think it affected him emotionally.

Meanwhile, we spent the summer of 1940 at our cottage again, but it was not as much fun. We were worried about my father, and I was anticipating going to school in the fall.

Me in front of a beauty shop on the first day of school.

When the time came, I got dressed in my best clothes. After break-fast, my mother presented me with a *Zuckertüte*. Like real candles on the Christmas tree, we don't have this tradition in the United States— giving every child a "sugar cone," covered with shiny paper and filled with chocolates and candy on the first day of school. It looks like an upside-down, princess hat and is supposed to "sweeten" the experience of leaving the safety of one's home. Mine was decorated with paper that had swirls in all the colors of the rainbow.

My mother accompanied me to the *Volksschule*, which served grades one to 14. The two-story, brick building was about two-thirds of a mile away on the Pankstrasse, so named because it crossed the Panke, Berlin's third-largest river (after the Havel and the Spree). I don't remember anything else about what happened that morning. From the next day on, I went by myself, taking a shortcut through an alley between two buildings across the street from our apartment house. Then, I walked over the bridge past a police station to the school.

Our class was on the first floor. We had two teachers. Mrs. Goloff taught history and Mr. Markbret taught everything else—German, math, writing, geography and more. By the time the second morning bell rang, we were in our seats waiting for Mr. Markbret. When he arrived, we stood up as one, gave the Hitler salute, right arm extended, and said in unison, "Good morning, Mr. Markbret. Heil Hitler."

He answered, "Heil Hitler. Sit."

For a while, he instructed us in religion, too. I had been placed in the Protestant class. I knew I was Lutheran, but that was all. No one in my family ever went to church on Sundays, at Christmas, or on any other holiday. We didn't kneel by the side of the bed to pray at night. Looking back, it seems odd, since so many people in America belong to one church or another. When people ask me now, I say I believe in God in my own way; and I pray at night for my children and my family.

The surface of our wooden desks slanted downward toward us. Beneath was an open space where we stored our books and notebooks. At the top was a narrow, flat board with a concave indentation for our pens. Next to it was a deeper cavity for ink. Between classes, the more mischievous boys who sat behind girls would dip the ends of their long pigtails in the ink wells and laugh uproariously. The next day those girls would come in with their hair pinned up. I was lucky. I rarely wore pigtails, and the boys didn't bother me.

I liked going to school and learning all kinds of new things. But what I liked even more was walking home past the house where my great-grandmother lived on Kösliner Strasse. She and her sister occupied a second-floor apartment above the hair salon. She was in her nineties and I didn't know her very well, but my mother told me that she used to babysit me every so often when I was little and my parents wanted to go to the movies. When I made a sound, she would take the nipple from a bottle, dip it in sugar, and put it in my mouth. According to my mother, when they got home, my face was all encrusted with sugar. For all I know, it is because of my great-grandmother that I have such a sweet tooth.

When she saw me coming down the street, she would lean out of the upstairs window and call to me. Then, she tossed a 50 Pfennig piece wrapped in newspaper down to the sidewalk. I yelled back, "Thank you," picked it up, and ran to the deli in our apartment building to buy macaroons. The Sawadas had three kinds—chocolate, vanilla, and strawberry—rolled in coconut shavings. I'd get one of each and take them to my secret hiding place beneath the foyer stairwell. There was a dark, hollow space underneath the landing leading up to the second floor. If I crouched there, nobody could see me. I didn't want to share my macaroons with anyone else, not Horst, not my mother. When I gobbled them down, they tasted like heaven.

Sometimes my sweet tooth got me in trouble. My father liked to make wine from red currants in the basement. One fall, after he finished a batch, he invited my aunts and uncles over to our apartment. When I asked for a taste, he poured me a small glass from the jug. I took a sip and it was sweet from the sugar he had used to make it. I downed the rest and asked for more. He gave me a look, but my uncle Kurt said, "Oh, go ahead, Erwin." So, my father poured me another glass. After I drank that, I got so tipsy I slid off the sofa. The next day at breakfast, I felt terrible. I must have looked like death warmed over because my father couldn't stop grinning.

At some point, a new girl came to the school and joined our class. She lived opposite from our apartment house on the Kösliner Strasse, in the same building where the coal dealer had his business. Her name was Eva Morgenstern. She had dark hair and brown eyes and was half a head shorter than me. Eva was rather shy and mostly kept to herself, remaining an outsider even during recess.

Eva on the right, me on the left.

One day, I introduced myself on the way to school. After that, we met up in the morning and walked to and from school together four times a day. We both came home for *Mittagessen*—the main meal of the day—and went back for the afternoon classes. On our way home, when we came around the corner from Pankstrasse, she would go one way, and I would head in the opposite direction. We were both school-oriented and talked about our lessons. She also asked me about our garden cottage—what vegetables we grew there and the animals we kept. It felt good to have a schoolmate like her.

In the late spring of 1941, my father was finally was released from the hospital for the last time. The doctors declared him cured and fit. Two weeks later, he was drafted into the army. It seemed so unfair. My mother's eyes were red-rimmed for days. I cried when he left. He gave us all a hug and promised to be back. But from the expression on my mother's face, I could tell she was worried sick.

My father in uniform.

We went to live in our cottage again that summer, but our mood was no longer sunny. With my father gone, my mother stopped breeding the rabbits, and their population started to dwindle. Whenever I went past the hutch, there were empty cages now, and I'd think of my father and wonder where he was.

Toward the end of June, the German army invaded Russia, and we were terribly worried for him. Finally, we received a postcard that he'd written from Czechoslovakia. It was plain and sand-colored—no picture on the front—just our address and the postage stamp. My mother was relieved—we all were—that he was alive.

Two of my uncles had been also been drafted. When we visited my aunts and mother's parents, we found out that Helmut was part of the campaign in northern Africa, and Kurt was fighting on the front lines in Russia. Everyone was worried about them. The only one who seemed happy was Werner, Oma Minna's son, who had become an SS paratrooper. A dedicated Nazi, he came to see her over the summer on a brief leave, excited to go on his first mission. I was amazed, listening to him talk about jumping out of airplanes with only a parachute to land behind enemy lines. I couldn't imagine what that was like.

When school started again, there was a lot of chatter about how well the war was going. Nazi flags were draped by the entrance and a picture of Adolf Hitler hung in the lobby. Most of my classmates had family members in the German army, navy, and air force. Some were proud and bragged about the military victories they'd heard about. So far, none had lost any relatives. For a while, we all settled into our daily routine.

One morning, I waited for Eva Morgenstern at the corner of Kösliner Strasse, but she didn't show up. When I got to school, she wasn't there either. At the midday meal, I told my mother about it, and she said that Eva probably stayed home because she was sick. After school, I was still worried about her, so my mother asked, "Do you want to go to her place and find out?"

I said, "Yes."

I had never been to Eva's apartment or met her mother and father. When we got there, it turned out that the Morgensterns lived on the first floor. The woman who opened the door wore a simple gray dress and apron. She had ash-blond hair tied in a bun. I could tell that she had been crying. A little boy peeked at us from behind her, holding on to her skirts. My mother introduced herself and Mrs. Morgenstern invited us in. The apartment was smaller than ours and smelled of boiled cabbage and caraway seeds. There was no one else inside.

We sat at the living room table and Mrs. Morgenstern told us that early in the morning, the Gestapo had knocked on the door and taken Eva and her husband away. Her lips were drawn tight and she kept staring into the air in front of her. The boy stood by her side with his head in her lap. My mother asked if there was anything we could do, but she shook her head. Then she thanked us for coming and got up. There was an awkward silence as she ushered us out. By the time I looked back, she had closed the door.

On the way home, I asked my mother, "What happened to my friend?"

My mother said, "I don't know. They need people to work and she's probably in a camp."

"But why?"

"Because they're Jews."

I felt so bad for Eva. Until that visit, I hadn't realized that she and her father were Jewish. I had never met anyone who was Jewish before. It wasn't until after the war ended that I found out about the concentration camps, mass deportations and executions, and how much Hitler hated Jews and was determined to kill them all. Such ignorance may seem hard to believe nowadays, but we didn't read newspapers, didn't have a radio, television, or the Internet where we lived. No one in my family, downstairs at the deli, at school, or in our summer cottage park ever talked about it.

But when we got back to our apartment, my mother took hold of my shoulders, looked me in the eyes, and said severely, "You can't talk to anyone about this. If we say anything against the government, they'll come and take us away, too."

Her ferocity scared me, and I promised I wouldn't. Thinking back now, I suspect she knew more than she let on. It was the only time I saw fear in her eyes.

Although I did what she demanded, I wondered why the Gestapo didn't take the little boy away, too. Perhaps, he came from a different marriage and was German like his mother so they left him alone. I never saw him or Eva's mother again. I imagine they moved away after what happened.

I think of Eva often. I like to believe that somehow she and her father didn't perish in the Holocaust, but I know that's wishful thinking. In all likelihood, they were among the six million Jewish victims of the Nazi regime.

3

Wartime

For the next year or so, our lives went on as before. To make ends meet, my mother started to clean and cook for the Sawadas during the week when they were busy running the store. She also cleaned for my granduncle Kuno, the banker. He had a one-bedroom, bachelor flat near the Kurfürstendamm on the second story of a fancy apartment building. I met him occasionally when my mother took me along on Saturdays. We had to travel by bus to get there. Uncle Kuno was stocky and a bit stiff and spoke very deliberately, pronouncing every syllable perfectly. He always had a fat cigar in his mouth. The smoke was slightly sweet, but it got into the furniture and drapes, and the whole apartment smelled like a train station. Although not unfriendly—he treated my mother well and gave us food when he had extra rations—he didn't pay much attention to me.

He died shortly after the war when he fell asleep with a burning cigar in his hands. His apartment caught on fire so quickly that the smoke and flames overcame him before he could get out, and he burned to death.

Sometimes, the Koehn family that lived upstairs from us would watch out for my brother and me. Mrs. Koehn, whose first name was Minna, like my grandmother, was at least twenty years older than my mother. She had once owned a restaurant. Now retired, she had her two grown daughters, who were still single and worked in a factory, living with her. Martha was a small, pudgy woman; her sister Charlotte was thinner. They were quite friendly and sometimes invited us children to join them for the midday meal when my mother was away. Their apartment was very cluttered because they saved everything—newspapers, magazines—but also spotless clean.

When the weather warmed up, we went to our cottage as before and spent time with my Opa Otto and Oma Minna. Occasionally she heard from her son, Werner. He always sent glowing reports of Nazi military successes.

On weekends, we visited family. Sometimes we would gather at the home of one of my uncles who wasn't fighting in the war. Aunt Ellie and Gertrude, the wives of Uncle Helmut and Uncle Kurt, joined us and shared any news they'd received from the front via letters and postcards.

We kids didn't participate in any of those conversations and only listened with half an ear, playing with our cousins in another room or outside. But as time went on, the optimism of the first year of the war yielded to somber news, and the mood became more subdued.

After the Japanese attack on Pearl Harbor on December 1941, Hitler declared war on the United States as well, and American forces landed in North Africa to support the British in the desert war there. Uncle Helmut, who was part of a tank brigade led by General Erwin Rommel, known as "the Desert Fox," was evidently involved in the fighting.

In the summer of 1942, we heard that a big battle had started in Russia at a city called Stalingrad, where Uncle Kurt was serving. I couldn't imagine what that was like, but I worried about my father. Postcards from him didn't come very often.

In 1943, allied airplanes attacked Berlin for the first time. None of the bombs fell near where we lived, although we all heard about it.

I have no memory of that raid. It was an isolated incident, and the planes returned only occasionally after that.

The other ways we realized that the war was not going as planned was more personal. Food and other household products were becoming scarce. We had no tooth paste and brushed our teeth with salt. The government poured all its resources into the military. With so many men fighting in different theaters of war and factories geared to manufacture war equipment, there weren't enough workers for the rest.

We were getting ration cards for food, but we couldn't buy enough with them. Fortunately, the Sawadas downstairs and their farming relatives continued to supply our neighborhood with plenty of vegetables.

Meanwhile, my brother started school, too, and we walked to and from our classes together. Most of our teachers were women and older men. Mr. Markbret wasn't there anymore. He'd been drafted into the army.

When I turned ten in 1944, I had to join the *Jungmädelbund*— Young Girls' League—the female equivalent of the Hitler Youth. The older teenagers, age 14 to 18, were in the *Bund Deutscher Mädels*— League of German Girls. We had to wear a uniform consisting of a dark blue skirt, white blouse, tie, and white knee socks. On Saturdays after school, we meet as a group, played games, marched carrying Nazi flags, and went on hikes in the Berlin forests—not my favorite activity. I was a city girl and didn't like to walk in the woods. It was a lot like girl scouts, but with Hitler salutes. Sometimes we'd gather and have to listen to women who gave talks about how great the *Führer* was and our glorious destiny as girls to become homemakers and mothers. Giving Hitler blond-haired, blue-eyed babies, preferably boys, didn't sound very inspiring to me.

Fortunately, I didn't have to go for long because the war took a turn for the worse. In 1944, allied air attacks on Berlin became more frequent; at first, only at night; but later, during the day as well. By then, we had put thick, blackout curtains over our windows at night so that no light would shine for the bombers to target. When we heard the alarm sirens—loud, piercing, high-pitched danger signals, which went on and on until I wanted to cover my ears—we would gather our things and head for the basement in our building. We stayed there until we heard the sirens sounding the all clear signal—three short blasts at a lower, less penetrating pitch than the alarm.

The British and American planes didn't just rain regular bombs from the skies. They also dropped bales of hay and phosphorous bombs with delayed detonators that would ignite after they hit the ground. Immediately, after the raid was over, my mother and the Sawadas would go up on the flat roof of our building to make sure no bundles of straw or hay had landed and burned there.

Once in a while, we'd be caught at school, or on our way there or back, and we'd run into the nearest building as fast as we could. As the raids became more frequent, we'd go to school in the morning only long enough to get our lessons, printed on cheap paper. We took them home, completed them, and brought them with us to school the next morning, and got new lessons.

One of the bombing attacks in the fall was so relentless and ferocious that we spent three days cooped up in the basement. It was dreary down there and the air smelled stale because there were no windows for circulation. Sometimes we lit a candle, but more often than not, we sat in the pitch-black bunker for hours on end. We had only chairs, no beds or cots to sleep on, and a bucket in a smaller area off to one side, so we could go to the bathroom with some privacy. It was cold down there even in the summertime, but we didn't feel it. My mother, worried that if bombs dropped on the building, we wouldn't be able to go back to our apartment. So, she made us wear four layers of clothing—one for each season. It was uncomfortable to sit bundled up like that, but at least we were warm.

When the bombs struck, the whole building shook, even during attacks on other parts of the city. We would grab the support pillars or each other and hold on for dear life. I gripped so hard that I never noticed if I felt scared. When the all clear sounded, we climbed upstairs, relieved and exhausted, and went to sleep.

After that three-day raid, the authorities canceled school permanently. Although we heard plenty of rumors about buildings being reduced to rubble and numerous people losing their lives, no one in my extended family was hurt.

Later that week, the police drove through the streets with bullhorns and ordered us to pack up our belongings and go to the train station. We were being evacuated from the city to the countryside, where it would be safer. We filled one suitcase with clothes, a few family pictures, and other belongings and rode to the station on the back of a truck. From there, a train took us to Luckenwalde, a small town about thirty miles south of Berlin.

It was late in October and we rode through forests whose trees had lost their leaves and along brown, harvested wheat fields and meadows where cows grazed. Luckenwalde was surrounded by farmland and woods, but it had some manufacturing plants, too. In the 1770s, cloth and wool factories had sprung up there, along with printing and dye works. By the 1920s, the town had developed a significant hat making industry. During the war, it also had a Stalag, a Nazi POW camp, which imprisoned Poles, Italians, and French, but no Russian soldiers. The inmates were forced to work in the factories, and thousands died because of the harsh labor conditions and not enough food.

I didn't know anything about that at the time. When we arrived at the Luckenwalde train station, local functionaries wearing red swastika armbands met us. They examined our identification papers with German efficiency and drove us to a two-story villa in a pleasant part of town. It belonged to an elderly gentleman, Mr. Hildebrandt, who had lost his wife due to illness. He lived upstairs with his daughter, Gisela, and her three children, two girls and a boy, who were all younger than me. Her husband had been drafted into the army, like my father, and was fighting somewhere on the western front. Having refugees like us stay at his house gave Mr. Hildebrandt a little extra income.

Our host welcomed us and showed us our room on the first floor near the kitchen. It had a bed, a dresser, a lamp, and a small table with two chairs. We were allowed to use the kitchen both to store provisions and to cook.

After we got settled my mother enrolled my brother and me in the local *Volksschule*, which was down the street within easy walking distance. Although we arrived nearly two months into the school year, the students there were considerably behind us. I soon realized that the teacher gave lessons I had completed earlier that year in Berlin. My classmates were just beginning to learn what I knew already, and I found school rather boring.

As in Berlin, the food rations didn't provide us with enough to eat, so my mother went to the surrounding farms and traded some of our belongings—sewing needles, a pair of scissors, threat for darning socks, and sewing on buttons—and our sugar rations for carrots, potatoes, and onions. Those were the staples we existed on for most of the war.

One day, a bomb crashed into a building that stored coffee. The news spread like wildfire through town. Everyone ran there and gathered as many of the raw coffee beans that had spilled everywhere as they could. When my mother came home with an apron full of the small, green, pea-sized beans, she roasted them in a pan on the stove. The aroma that filled the kitchen reminded me of our happier life before the war when my father was still with us. I loved the smell, but it also made me sad. My mother ground a few of the beans in the coffee mill and made one cup for herself and one for our host, a treat after the *Ersatzkaffee*—the coffee substitute, which consisted of malt, grains, and chicory. The rest she traded away for food for us. She even gave me a taste, but I found it too bitter for my liking.

As we became regular members of the community, my mother even started saving accounts for my brother and me at the local bank. I still have the savings book in my possession, and it shows a small balance, but I don't know what happened to the money when we left town. Perhaps my mother withdrew it and took it with her but never told me about it.

At Christmas, she tore a few branches off a pine tree and hung them in our room. There were no ornaments for decorations. My mother had managed to save an apple and an orange, and those were our presents that year. When it snowed, we built a snowman in the yard. We found some dark pebbles for his eyes, nose and mouth. We didn't give him the traditional carrot nose. Food was too precious to waste that way.

From left to right: Horst, Frieda, Sophie, and me.

With the dawning of the new year, the reality that Germany had lost the war became inescapable. The allied propeller planes rumbled overhead on their way to bombing Berlin, Leipzig, and Dresden.

Leipzig was only 50 miles to the southwest, and we watched it burning one February night, the dark sky glowing red and gold above the horizon. Dresden was too far away for us to see, but we felt the ground shaking from the host of firebombs raining down on that doomed city.

Rumors of American, British, and Russian troops advancing on Berlin from all sides grew dire. By then, Russian armies had crossed the Oder River and were pushing deep into German territory. Before long, they attacked Luckenwalde, and we hid in the basement of the villa while local troops put up a vigorous defense. The mayor refused to concede, and for two days the battle raged, with the Russians taking the town and the German armies taking it back several times. But in the end, it was a lost cause and the mayor hoisted the white flag of surrender on top of city hall.

A little more than two weeks later, on May 7, 1945, the German government capitulated to the allies. The Nazi dream of a thousand-year Reich was finished.

The war in Europe was over. But our hardships were not.

4

War's Aftermath

The Russian armies did not come as liberators as much as conquerors, and they exacted their revenge on the civilian population. Soldiers went into homes to loot and take away anything of value they could find. They drove up and down the streets with their trucks to pick up German women and rape them.

We lived close to the railroad tracks and watched the trains go by as they headed east, Russia bound. The flatbed cars were filled with farm animals and industrial machinery from the factories in the region. We found out later that such relentless plundering went on all over the German territory controlled by the Russians.

One time, a young soldier came into the villa carrying a hand full of potatoes he'd dug up in someone's garden. They were still covered with soil. Dressed in uniform and boots, he wore a hat with ear flaps down even though it wasn't cold. We kids were curious and followed him around, all five of us. When he found the bathroom, he threw the potatoes into the toilet to wash off the dirt. German toilets had water tanks mounted high up on the wall instead of behind the bowl. There was a pull chain with small metal links, and the soldier yanked on it. Down the pipe the water came rushing and flushed all the potatoes away with a gurgle. The soldier stood there, flabbergasted. We couldn't help but laugh.

We weren't afraid—he looked more surprised than angry—and kept following him as he made his way around the house. In the living room, he found a ceramic sugar bowl on the dining room table. He took a curtain rod lying by the window, dipped it into the bowl, and licked the sugar off. Then, he went into the basement to look around further. Glass jars filled with canned fruit and vegetables lined a wooden shelf. There were quite a few. The soldier took one look at them and swept his rod across the shelf. All the jars fell to the concrete floor, cracking and breaking with a sickening sound. Glass shards, liquid, beets, pickles, peaches, and pears spilled everywhere. It was a mean-spirited act of destruction and revenge so we wouldn't have anything to eat either.

Another time, three soldiers came to the house and looked around but didn't find anything they wanted. As they left, one of them muttered something in Russian, and Mr. Hildebrandt understood that he was asking, "What time is it?" So, he took out his gold pocket watch to check, and the soldier grabbed it from him. Mr. Hildebrandt came back inside in tears—it was a keepsake his wife had given him, and now it was gone. I had never seen a man cry before, and the memory has stayed with me for over seventy years.

Whenever the local baker got a supply of flour, he'd bake bread. When my mother found out, she'd blacken her face with coal and put on an apron with a torn pocket to make herself look unattractive to the Russian soldiers. Then, she went to the shop and waited outside with all the others who had assembled. At some point, the baker would open the door and toss the loaves into the crowd. If you were lucky, you'd catch one. My mother never did. Instead, she continued to go around to farms to barter for food. We worried for her safety. Fortunately, she always came back unharmed.

At night, Russian soldiers patrolled the streets or walked around town in groups, singing songs at the top of their voices after getting drunk. They'd come up to the houses and shine flashlights into the windows. Since we lived on the first floor, we experienced that a lot. We had pushed our bed against the far wall. My brother slept on the outer edge with me in the middle and my mother against the wall so the Russians couldn't see her.

Our host had a large shed next to the house with a false ceiling under the roof. Some nights, my mother and Gisela would climb up there to hide, and my brother and I shared the bed by ourselves. We didn't go to sleep until very late because the soldiers made such a racket. We never felt afraid, though. The Russians left children alone.

That didn't mean I survived that time unscathed. In anticipation of the surrender, my mother had me take off the coral earrings my grandmother Ellie had given me. She was afraid that some soldier would tear them from my ear lobes. So, she wrapped them up and put them in a box along with our other valuables, which included a knife with an ivory handle my father had taken from a Hungarian soldier and sent to us. Next to the front doorsteps of the house was an iron grate where we scuffed our shoes before going inside. My mother lifted that grate and buried the box in the sand underneath, hoping that no one would bother to look there.

But wouldn't you know it, the Russians were smarter than that. One member of a search party carried a saber and stuck it through the grate into the sand and found the box. He took everything in it, along with my earrings. I cried for a day, inconsolable over the loss.

Late in June, when things calmed down, my mother started to wonder out loud if our house in Berlin was still standing. Finally, she said, "Let's go home."

We packed our few belongings into my doll carriage, putting my father's leather coat, which was precious to my mother, on the bottom. In the early evening, we said our good-byes to Mr. Hildebrandt,

Gisela, and her children, and took off. We set out along the raised bed of railroad tracks that led to Berlin. It was early summer and not too chilly. When it got dark, the bright moon lit our way. We pulled the carriage behind us across the railway ties. It was a bumpy journey and we had to proceed with care so we wouldn't trip and tumble down the embankment.

We weren't alone. Other refugees were going back to Berlin, too. Some carried old suitcases which they had tied up with hemp rope; others had hardly any belongings. We all traveled at night. During the day, we hid from the Russians in the woods by the side of the tracks and napped as best we could.

It took us four days to walk to Berlin. By then, several railroad lines had converged. As we got close to Potsdam and passed a train station, I saw two men leaning against the building. They were eating bread. When my brother and I ran up to them, they broke off two small chunks and gave them to us. We wolfed them down.

Then a passenger train arrived. My mother found out where it was headed and told us to get on. We rode for a while and got off at Babelsberg, where my Aunt Margaret and Uncle Alfred lived with their four children. We passed bombed-out residences on the way to their place on the fourth floor of an apartment building, but most of their neighborhood was still intact.

When we got there, Aunt Grete welcomed us with open arms. She was pregnant with her fifth child and close to her due date. We spent three days at her house, washed our clothes and enjoyed a bath in their bathtub, cleaning off the dirt and grime from our long walk. They had a vegetable garden out backs. My aunt made a big stew and flavored it with parsley. It smelled so good and tasted even better.

My aunt was glad to see us because my uncle was in prison. By then, the allies had divided Berlin into four sectors—American, Russian,

British and French. Babelsberg on the east side of the city was in the Russian zone. My uncle, who was a house painter, rode his bicycle to the other zones to paint people's apartments. They paid him in German West Marks, which he exchanged for East Marks at a 4:1 rate. The extra money made it easier for him to support his family. But jealous neighbors informed the Russian authorities—my aunt knew the people that had done it, but she wouldn't say who they were. I think she was afraid what would happen to her if they found out she told on them.

One day, after my uncle exchanged some money, the police and Russians picked him up and threw him in jail. When my aunt found out, she went to the police station and asked why and when he would come home. But they never said and kept him locked up.

By the time we got to my aunt's house, he had been incarcerated for some time. He was not getting much food and became thin as a rail. Five weeks after we left her, we received news that he had died in prison. My aunt was left all alone with five children. My oldest cousin, Joachim, who was two years younger than me, helped her by doing odd jobs. Eventually, he became a painter as well. Fortunately, their garden was plentiful, which helped them survive.

We were there when my aunt went into labor, and my mother helped her deliver the baby. I was in the bedroom when my cousin was born. He looked like a naked bird, his arm skinny and thin as pins. Against all odds, he survived. Berndt was my aunt's last child and, the funniest one of the five. As he got older, whenever he started talking, he soon had everybody in stitches. He died just three years before this book was written.

When we were sure that he and my aunt would be okay, we left to go home to our apartment. It was another long walk, and we passed many buildings that had been destroyed by the bombing raids. In retrospect, it occurred to me that so many of those air attacks were deliberately directed at the civilian population, not any military or industrial targets. Like the firebombing of Dresden and Hamburg, they were atrocities inflicted on ordinary German people, not soldiers, not die-hard Nazis. Although the rules of war supposedly protect the innocent, civilians always suffer. That was as true then as it is now.

We reached Wedding, which was in the French sector, in the late afternoon. The closer we got to our street, the more anxious my mother became, and by the time we turned the corner into Weddingstrasse, she was a nervous wreck. The houses on either side of the street were bombed out. Some of the brick walls still stood like bare ruins, but the floors had collapsed, and there were mountains of rubble and debris everywhere. We later found out that an airplane spiraling out of control had flattened the kiosk column at the corner and smashed into apartment house number 5.

Miraculously, our corner building was still standing. As we got closer, we noticed that all the windows were broken or boarded up. We made our way up the steps and inside to the foyer. The wooden staircase had new support beams holding it up. On the mezzanine, the floor wobbled, and we kept to the wall, afraid that it might collapse if we walked in the middle.

The door to our apartment was locked. When we opened it and went inside, it was as we had left it, except that all the windows had been blown out. Surprisingly, the electricity worked. Happy to be home in familiar surroundings, we didn't bother to unpack. Even though it was cold inside, we collapsed on the beds and slept through the night.

The next day we discovered that the Koehns upstairs had come back already, and the Seibarts as well. There were only women and children in the apartment house, no men. When we asked around what we should do about our windows, people told us to board them up. We had a large birch cupboard in the living room, and my mother took off the back with a screwdriver and a claw hammer. Then she nailed the wooden sheet to the window frame. It was large enough to cover the gaping hole. The back of a dresser worked just as well for the bedroom window.

We had a little coal left in the basement, so we could cook on the stove in the kitchen. When we ran out, we took some of our wooden furniture apart—chairs and bedside tables—and used them to stoke the cooking fire. Later, my mother and an older man, who lived downstairs on the Kösliner Strasse side of our building and hadn't been drafted, would go to Grünewald, a large forested area in West Berlin. They'd cut down a small tree, lug it in a big potato sack to our building, and saw it into pieces in the courtyard in back. It would take them all day.

One time, I asked her, "Mama, how can you carry all that heavy wood home?"

She gritted her teeth and said, "I'm not doing it for myself."

As we settled in, my mother took charge as best she could, resuming her duties as building manager. There was no garbage pickup, so people just threw their trash into the rubble, even though there were empty waste cans in the back of the building. The stench was horrible. Whenever my mother saw someone dumping garbage, she yelled at them to put it into the bins, but only a few listened. Soon we had an infestation of rats who had a picnic with the refuse among the piles of bricks, splintered boards, and wooden beams. They were fearless and a health hazard—they bit people—and my mother was responsible for getting rid of them. She put out traps at night. In the morning, she'd take the dead rats she'd caught and toss them into the empty barrels.

At night, bed bugs bothered us. There were so many and they sucked the blood out of us. When we turned over, we'd squash them, and they stained the sheets with red splotches. Everybody had them.

When the Sawadas came back, everyone was happy to see them. There were hugs and kisses all around. They reopened their deli and started to sell some vegetables, flour, and other groceries. We received food rations for butter, sugar, and bread.

As German soldiers came back from the front and prisoners returned who had survived the concentration camps, there were guarded conversations about what had happened. The Sawadas, with their outgoing personalities made it easier for people to talk.

One day, I overheard Mrs. Sawada say to a well-dressed woman wearing gold earrings and a gold necklace, "Why, you still have your jewelry!"

The woman said, "Yes, when I heard the Russians were coming and stealing everything, I put them into my little *Mausie*," and pointed to the area below her belly.

I went upstairs and asked my mother what the woman meant by that. She looked at me suspiciously and asked, "Where did you hear that?"

I said, "A customer downstairs said that."

My mother shrugged. "Well, you're old enough now to know about that." Then, she explained to me how some women used to hide their jewelry in their vagina, and added, "A number of women I know did that."

I wish I had known about that earlier. I would have done it, too, with my coral earrings.

The butcher said there was no regular meat—the Russians had taken all the farm animals from the surrounding countryside. But he had horse meat from the animals that pulled the beer wagons and had been slaughtered. He turned it into sausage, salami, and smoked ham. My mother brought some home and made goulash. The meat was redder than beef and very lean. She used lard in the pan to brown it. It smelled so good and tasted good, too. I liked it better than the deer meat we'd had in Luckenwalde, and it sustained us for a while.

My mother also did laundry, cooked, and cleaned for the Sawadas again. When their farm relatives sent them potatoes, she would grate them to make salted potatoes and bring the peels upstairs with her. We'd put them through the coffee grinder, and she'd make potato pancakes for us.

But we often went hungry because there was not enough food. The Russians, determined to starve Berlin's population, refused to allow the farmers to bring produce into the city. So, my mother took the little rations of sugar we received and small kitchen items and traveled by train into the countryside, knocked on the farmers' doors to trade them for food. She'd come back with potatoes, carrots, and onions. They made for lean fare, but that's how we survived.

There were so many people on the trains that sometimes my mother would have to sit on the roof. As they came close to a tunnel, people up ahead would yell out a warning, and everybody ducked.

Sometimes, she didn't come home at night, and my brother and I huddled under the blankets to keep warm. The wood covering the windows didn't keep out the cold. I wasn't afraid. I trusted that she would return, and she always did.

To make additional money, my mother worked on weekends to reclaim bricks from the bombed-out houses. She'd put on heavy gloves to remove the mortar and cement with a pointed hammer so that the bricks could be used again. It was hard work, and she came home exhausted, but I never heard her complain. In retrospect, I am still amazed by what she did to take care of us.

Every now and so often, my mother tried to find out what happened to my father. His postcards had stopped coming in 1944. But we never received news of his being captured or dying on the battlefield.

As a result, my mother refused to believe that he was gone. "Until I find out otherwise, I know he is alive," she insisted.

My mother also wanted to find out if her parents in Moabit were okay. There were no trams or buses yet, so we had to walk. At some point, we had to cross a bridge which had slid into the canal. All that was left above the waterline were the concrete railing on one side and a narrow section of sidewalk. We had to edge along, stepping carefully, first my mother, then my brother, and then me. We made it safely across and walked to my cousin Reinhardt's apartment. His parents, Opa Kurt and Oma Augusta, were staying with him because their place had been bombed out. We were glad they were all right.

The next time we went to see them, the S-Bahn—Berlin's elevated subway—was running again and we rode it to Moabit. We went with Oma and Opa to their old house to see what if anything still remained. Half the building and the entire front had been torn away so we could see into the apartments. On the fourth floor where they had lived, right under the roof of the building, the only thing that was left of their living room was a wall with a large grandfather clock. All of a sudden, the floor gave way and the clock came crashing down, making a hollow, clanging sound when it hit the ground and its wooden casing broke apart. We all screamed because it happened so unexpectedly. It was like an omen, a traumatic event for my grandparents. They'd lost everything—all their furniture, belongings, and most of their clothes—and when that clock came down, it felt like their life was over even though they lived for another ten years.

When we visited our other relatives, we discovered that Uncle Helmut had returned unharmed from Africa, although he never talked about his experiences at the battle of El Alamein and afterward.

Uncle Kurt had been less fortunate. We knew he had fought in the Battle of Stalingrad, not in the city but in an area immediately to the south. As the situations became dire, orders came to retreat and the German Air Force began to evacuate the soldiers. When the last plane was about to leave, my uncle wanted to climb aboard but was told there was no more room. As the aircraft started to take off, he hung onto a wing and begged them to take him along. One of the soldiers pried his hands off, and he fell to the ground. He was never heard from again.

One of his comrades who'd managed to get a seat on the plane visited my aunt and told her the sad story. I felt so bad for him and my aunt, Gertrude. Apparently, he never knew that he had another daughter. The last time he had been on leave, he'd gotten my aunt pregnant. After my cousin Brigitte was born, my aunt wrote him, but she had no idea if he ever received her letter.

Meanwhile, my mother continued to barter for food. While she was away, the Koehns upstairs kept an eye out for my brother and me. The three women liked me a lot. Once Martha sewed me an embroidered dress. Another time, she made a velvet burgundy coat for me. They also tried to teach me to play the piano, but I never got the hang of it. They had better success showing me the proper way to eat dinner with a fork and knife. When my brother and I went upstairs, they always gave us something to eat.

Mrs. Koehn probably saved my life. I carried a chain with a key around my neck for the cupboard where we kept our food rations. We could eat two slices of bread each day, and I was supposed to dole them out when my mother was away. But Horst was always hungry, and one time he wanted my share. When I refused, he got so angry he tried to push me out of the living room window.

By then, our windows had been replaced, which made our apartment more comfortable and brighter during the day. In the sweltering heat, we kept them open to catch the summer breezes. The bottom of the frame reached down to a low window seat. Horst shoved me from behind and kept pushing. I managed to hang on the window frame, screaming bloody murder. Mrs. Koehn heard me, rushed downstairs, and shouted for Horst to stop. Then she took us both to her apartment and watched us until my mother came home and her daughters returned from work.

I expected my mother to lay into my brother for what he tried to do to me, but she looked exhausted and didn't have the energy to punish him. He never apologized and we continued on as if it had never happened.

When we visited our garden cottage that summer, we found out that Oma's son Werner, the paratrooper, had disappeared without a trace, too. Although the area was now under French control, immediately after the German surrender, the Russians had stolen all of her animals—chickens, ducks, geese, goats, and sheep. It annoyed her to no end, but she insisted she would get new ones as soon as she could; and she did. We were glad that the Russians didn't find my father's motorcycle, which we had hidden in the garden house under covers to make it look like a large box.

When my mother heard that there was a shortage of tobacco, she decided to plant a dozen or so plants at our cottage. By the fall, they had matured and grown big, green leaves. We harvested them, laid them flat on a wooden table and sprinkled sugar water on them. When they turned dark brown, we stacked them and carried them to the tobacco merchant on our street. He had a machine to cut the leaves into strands so you could make cigarettes. He also sold us rolling paper. My mother and I took the tobacco and papers to the black market. We'd ask passersby "Tobacco?" and when one would nod and answer, "Potatoes, flour," we would go into the entrance of an apartment building to haggle and make the exchange.

At some point, school started up again.

We didn't have enough teachers, so the classes were overcrowded. By then, I was twelve, and my classroom was on the second floor—all girls. The boys had their separate room across the hall. After school, we'd play kickball in the street. It was still boys against girls, and we continued to lose. Some of my older teammates started to make eyes at the teenage boys, although I never did.

When it rained, I'd walk to school with an umbrella. In the winter, it was harder because I didn't have boots. The snow was wet and cold and got into my shoes. One time, I developed frostbite on my right heel. My mother didn't know what to do. When she happened to mention it to a customer in the deli, the woman said, "Here's how you treat it. When the beer wagon comes by, pick up some of the horse droppings. Then put them in a bowl and pour boiling water over them. Have Trauty soak her feet in it when she can tolerate the heat."

We tried the remedy and it worked. The horse apples didn't even smell once they were submerged in water. I recovered, but ever since, the heel bone on my right foot sticks out a little, more than on the left, although I can walk just fine. It is my personal war memento.

As I was getting older, I became curious about what had happened during the Nazi era and why. But we didn't learn anything about it in school. None of the teachers wanted to talk about the war or the years before. So, I started to buy newspapers and magazines to find out what I could. I saw some photos of concentration camps and the inmates in their striped clothing looking gaunt as ghosts as they were being starved to death. I was so shocked I wanted to shut my eyes, but I made myself look. That was what Hitler did to my friend Eva Morgenstern and her father. He wanted to kill all the Jews.

I was glad he took poison in his bunker, a miserable failure, along with Goebbels and his family. I read about the Nuremberg Trials, and

Rudolf Hess being incarcerated in Spandau Prison for the rest of his life. I also learned about how scared people were to say anything against Hitler and the Nazis, even at home, because they were afraid their own children and neighbors would turn them in. I could not imagine doing that to my mother or brother.

After I came to America and watched television, I found out even more horrible things that had happened during the Holocaust.

At the time, I wrote an essay about everything I had discovered. When I showed it to the principal, who was also my teacher, she said, "Oh, Waltraut, we have to exhibit this so all the students can read it. She had it printed up on two large pages backed by cardboard and displayed it in the front entrance to the schools.

When my mother heard about it, she was proud of me but looked at me with regret and said, "You didn't have much of a childhood, Trauty, did you."

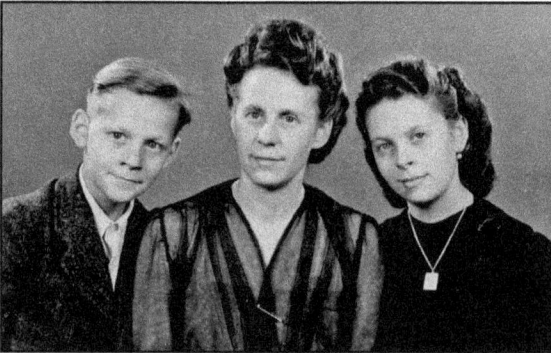

Horst, my mother and I at my confirmation in 1948.
My mother is wearing a dress made from parachute material.

5

Homecoming

As German soldiers returned from the eastern front, my mother kept wondering about what had happened to my father. At some point, the Red Cross forwarded a postcard from him—she recognized his handwriting. Russian soldiers had captured him in eastern Hungary and taken him to a prison camp somewhere in Siberia, but he was all right. She tried to find out more, but that's all the authorities could tell her. She even went to a Gypsy who looked into her crystal ball and confirmed that he was alive.

Meanwhile, to help feed the German population, schools were giving out soup. After I had lunch at our apartment, I took an empty, metal milk can with me and brought it back home after school filled with soup. My mother would heat it up for our supper. It was watery and thin and tasted salty, but the small pieces of meat that floated among the carrots and turnips provided extra nourishment.

One afternoon, I started down the stairs from the mezzanine carrying the empty can and saw a man in the lobby. He was wearing a fur hat with the ear flaps lowered and a green felt army overcoat. He turned to come upstairs and looked up. It was my father!

My heart leapt in my chest, and I let out a scream and cried out, "Papa, Papa, Papa!"

All the apartment doors opened and the occupants came out to see what was happening. When they realized who it was, they all rushed downstairs and gathered around my father, welcoming him home. I had my arms around his waist and didn't mind being crushed by the others. My father meant everything to me, and he was back safe and sound.

When he took off his hat and coat in our apartment, we were shocked how bloated and swollen his face looked. For some reason, he had retained a lot of water after being released from the camp in Russia. His legs and ankles were so swollen that, when he lay on the couch and my brother and I pushed on his skin with our thumbs, we would make deep indentations. We later learned that a lot of prisoners came home like that.

After a doctor gave him injections, my father gradually recovered and returned to normal. He could put on the shoes he'd worn before the war again. He had survived for three years on boiled fish heads, cabbage soup, and a daily slice of bread. Things had been so bad for everyone in the surrounding region that the Russian people who lived nearby came up to the wire fences of the prison camp and begged him and his fellow inmates for food. He had brought back a few photos of us that he'd kept, but they were as thin as onion paper because he had peeled the back off so he could roll cigarettes.

*The picture of my mother which my father
carried with him during his imprisonment.*

My mother took brown paper and glued it on the back of the photos to reinforce them, but she couldn't get rid of the wrinkled appearance. I still have some of them.

My father didn't want to talk about his camp experiences, but I was nosy and kept pestering him until he'd say, "*Rutch mir mal den Buckel runter!*—Get lost!" (Literally: "Go slide down my back!"). But I didn't let up. I wanted to know.

One Sunday afternoon, when he took a nap lying on his side, I noticed a red welt on the back of his neck. It looked like an upside-down letter L. When he woke up, I kept after him until he told me how he'd gotten it.

He had been sent to turn wheat stalks lying in a field to make sure they wouldn't rot. They'd been cut but not yet harvested. The pants he wore were tied at the bottom against the cold, and he took some of the kernels and hid them there. At night in the barracks, concealed under his sleeping blanket, he chewed on them. But some of the other prisoners heard him and ratted him out. The Russian guards came, threw him into a hole in the ground, and put a wooden lid on top.

After a day, one of the soldiers took the cover off. He carried a board with a nail sticking out. As my father tried to climb out of the hole, the soldier hit him over the back to punish him further, tearing a deep gash in his neck. Another guard wrapped a bandage around the bleeding wound and threw my father back in the hole. He stayed there for another day and half. He was lucky that the injury didn't get infected.

When he finished telling me, I burst into tears. It was so mean and cruel. He was starving! For many years, when I related that story to others, I always teared up.

Food was still scarce in Berlin. By then, my father had recovered enough and tried to take over for my mother, traveling to farms outside the city to barter for food. But after the first time, when he came home with only a handful of potatoes, he said to my mother, "Mama"—he always called her that—"Mama, I can't do this."

So, my mother resumed scrounging for food. She always came back with something, even if it was only a few red beets or a head of cabbage. She'd make warm sauerkraut and potatoes with caraway seeds. I hated the way they tasted and tried to pick them out, but the flavor remained. The Sawadas who had known us for twenty years were kind, setting food aside for us. The vegetable garden at our summer cottage and plums from our tree also helped.

Still, things got worse in early summer of 1948 when the Russians blocked all road, railway and canal access to the sectors of Berlin under Western control. The Soviet government was upset that the Allies had introduced a new German Mark and didn't want them to use it in West Berlin.

But their plan failed because the Allies organized the Berlin Airlift, known by us as *Die Luftbrücke* (the Air Bridge). For more than a year, they supplied the people of West Berlin with food and fuel. Plane after plane would land at Tempelhof Airport. Crews unloaded the provisions and stored them in empty hangers to distribute to the American, British, and French sectors. Soon, the Sawadas had sugar, margarine, butter in boxes in their store, and our local bakers received flour to make bread, all of which we could all buy with our food stamps.

Because the rations included little packs of raisins for us children, we called the cargo planes *Rosinenbomber* (Raisin Bombers)—the Americans referred to them as Candy Bombers. When we heard the drone of the planes overhead coming from the west, getting ready to land, we'd look up and say, "Here comes more food. I wonder what it'll be—maybe oranges!"

The *Luftbrücke* was a godsend for us. Organized by Americans, it involved the air forces of the United States, Britain, Canada, France,

Australia, and New Zealand. They flew over 200,000 missions, bringing nearly 13,000 tons of provisions a day until the Soviets lifted their blockade. A lot of Americans and many young Germans don't know about the Berlin airlift. It saved our lives at a time when the Russians wanted us to starve to death. I will always be grateful to the Americans whose generosity and can-do spirit helped us survive.

I want to take a moment to say something about my feelings toward Russians. My own experiences of Russian soldiers and the Soviet occupying forces of East Berlin were without exception negative, and many of my stories reflect that. It has taken me some time to realize that they don't represent all of the Russian people, and I don't mean to imply that I blame everyone for what happened then. At a time of widespread prejudice and racism, it's important not to make blanket accusations against an entire people and culture for the misdeeds of individuals.

As factories reopened, my father went back to work at Siemens. That allowed my mother to stay home and do the cooking, washing, and ironing. My father helped out in the winter, getting salt and sand from the basement to throw on the sidewalk when it iced over. He couldn't ride his motorcycle as before because he had difficulty breathing in the cold air. So, he sold it and bought a scooter instead. It didn't go as fast, but it got him to work and to our garden house just fine.

There were wild rabbits in the fields surrounding the Siemens factory. From time to time, my father would catch one, bring it home in his knapsack, and put it in one of the cages in the basement. After replenishing his supply, my father read up on how to cure and tan rabbit fur. Then he made a black pillbox hat for my mother, with black fur all around the side. He also bought fabric and sewed a burgundy coat for her as a Christmas present and lined the bottom with strips of rabbit fur. It was beautiful and elegant-looking.

My father was one of the few men I've known who could use a sewing machine. He had learned how to make clothes from his mother, using sheets of newspaper to create the patterns. He taught me how to do it, too, cut out the fabric pieces, and sew them together. I made a lot of my clothes.

One time, he bought my mother a pair of red shoes which showed off her legs. That year, they celebrated New Year's Eve in a restaurant. After drinking plenty of wine, my mother climbed on a table and showed off the shoes and her legs while performing the popular song "*Das Machen nur die Beine von Dolores*" ("That's What the Legs of Dolores Do").

Well, that didn't sit well with my father. He was a jealous man and became angry. As they arrived at home, he yelled at her so loud, accusing her of all kind of bad behavior, that everyone in the building woke up. I heard every word and cowered in the bedroom, hoping their fight would blow over. It did, although my mother didn't apologize and kept right on wearing those red shoes whenever she felt like it.

In the meantime, I graduated from *Volksschule*. My classmate Kate Schröder and I had been good students, and the teachers said that we should attend *Hochschule*, prep school for university. It was an honor, but my parents didn't have the money required, so I couldn't go. Kate's father had had an accident at work and received workman's compensation, so her family had the money to send her there. I was disappointed but not for long.

Although my brother had still two years to go, he skipped school a lot and got involved with a gang of hoodlums. They went into bombed out buildings and stole the copper plumbing pipes from apartments, which they sold on the black market. Then, they bought booze and got drunk at all hours of the day. At some point, they got caught, and Horst ended up spending time in jail. My father had to bail him out and went with him to the sentencing. Because Horst was still a minor and it was his first offense, the judge decided to be lenient and let him off with time served. But it was hard on my parents and hurt my father a lot.

Horst never earned his diploma. He was a talented painter who drew murals on the walls of apartments houses that everyone admired. He also built cornices and valences for windows and covered them with fabric. After a year of trade school, he became a house painter. But he never really straightened out, even though he got married and had four children. He continued to drink his money away and became verbally abusive toward my parents and his family.

I think my father's absence as a soldier and after the war, and my mother having to work so hard to keep us afloat, left Horst feeling alone and isolated and without the love he needed during his formative years. In some ways, he was as much a victim of the war as so many other civilians who remained traumatized by their experiences, suffering nightmares and emotional aftershocks.

But there was something deeply troubling inside him, too, an irrational anger, which I had experienced first-hand when he tried to push me out the window of our apartment. Unfortunately, his behavior affected others as well later on who had done nothing to deserve being mistreated by him.

6

Working

Since I couldn't go to *Hochschule*, I had to find a job. I thought about becoming a beautician, having checked out the hair salon across the street, but they didn't have an opening.

One afternoon, I went window shopping along the Badstrasse, a double-lane shopping street with a median in the middle. It crossed the Pankstrasse not too far from my school and turned south toward the Gesundbrunnen neighborhood, also known as *Die Plumpe* (the pump), where we went to catch the S-Bahn and city buses. As I passed a leather goods shop next to a bakery, I couldn't help but glance at the attractive gloves and purses displayed in the window. On a hunch, I went inside. Gerloff & Sienholz was an old, well-established store. There were suitcases on shelves, handbags hanging on dark, wooden walls, and gloves and travel kits displayed under the glass-topped counters. I liked the earthy leather smell.

As I looked around, an older woman in a light brown smock with the name of the store embroidered on the front came up to me and asked if she could help me. Without thinking, I blurted out, "I just graduated from school and am looking for work."

She didn't seem surprised but examined me more closely. Then she said, "Come with me."

I followed her to the back where three steps led up to a raised office area overlooking the store with shelves that held additional leather purses and pocketbooks. Behind a large, dark rosewood desk sat a middle-aged man with a friendly face. He looked up and said, "What is it, Mrs. Radomsky?"

She replied, "Mr. Sienholz, this young woman here is looking for a job."

The man eyed me curiously and asked, "What is your name, Miss?"

"Waltraut Kleiber. I live on Weddingstrasse not too far from here."

After giving me a more serious look-over, he asked me about my parents—what my father did—my school grades, and why I wanted to be a salesclerk. I didn't feel intimidated by him. On the contrary, he was easy to talk to, and I chattered away uninhibitedly.

Finally, he said, smiling, "When can you start?"

I was stunned but recovered quickly and said, "Monday morning."

Nodding, he explained the terms of my employment. I would earn 60 Marks a month. Store hours were from nine in the morning to seven at night with a one-hour lunch break, and half days on Saturday. There was one stipulation. They would not be able to send me to trade school because the store had only one slot and it had gone to girl he'd hired two weeks earlier. If I was okay with that, the job was mine. When I eagerly accepted, he asked Mrs. Radomsky to fit me with a smock before I left, and that was it!

I walked out of the shop as if floating on air and rushed home to share the good news with my parents. They were thrilled. Gerloff & Sienholz was a well respected business, founded by the Gerloff family in the 1800s. By the time I went to work there, the founders no longer ran the store. After Mr. Sienholz's father married into the family, they changed the name of the business. Now his son ran it. He was married and had a daughter a few years younger than me.

I worked for Gerloff & Sienholz for six years. There were three salesgirls, including Mrs. Radomsky, who was in charge of us and operated the cash register. Although I couldn't go to trade school to learn more about the leather business, I kept my ears peeled and found out as much as could from the other salesgirls.

For the midday break, I walked to our apartment and ate lunch with my mother and brother. Then I returned to the store for the rest of the day. On Saturday, I took my sales smock home and washed it for the next week.

I started out selling suitcases and quickly got the hang of it, graduating to ladies' gloves and purses. I liked working behind the counter and talking to customers. Because I had an interest in decorating and making things pretty, I crumpled up newspaper and stuffed it into a pair of gloves to make it look like there were hands inside, and arranged them to hold one of the pocketbooks. When Mr. Sienholz saw my display, he was impressed.

The store had a decorator for the big front window and the two display boxes mounted on either side of the entrance. At some point, a salesclerk took a purse from the window display because a customer wanted it and we didn't have another one like it in back. Mr. Sienholz asked me to replace it with a different pocketbook, and I climbed into the window with another pocketbook. While putting it on the cloth-covered stand, I rearranged the display more to my liking. When his wife saw what I had done, she let the decorator go and asked me to take care of the displays after that.

I was happy to do it even though it meant staying after hours some evenings, and I didn't get paid extra. It made me feel important and proud that they appreciated my abilities.

In December, the store also opened on Sundays from two in the afternoon until six for Christmas shopping. When it was time for a break, Mr. Sienholz went across the street to the frankfurter stand and bought hot dogs with mustard for us.

The Christmas after I started to decorate the windows, he gave me a present, a 10-Mark bonus.

I liked working there, except when Mr. Sienholz's aunt came into the store. She was the last remaining Gerloff. Her hair was gray and her thin lips drawn tight as if she wanted to make sure she wouldn't accidentally smile. She positioned herself behind us and watched as we looked after costumers. When we were done, she took us aside and criticized our performance, saying, "Next time, stand up straighter," or, "Hold the pocketbook more to the side so they can see it better." She always found fault with something we'd done, and we were happy when she left.

Mr. Sienholz, on the other hand, was a good boss. He was very educated and handsome, but he had problems with his stomach, which required him to eat fruit. In the morning, after he'd settled behind his desk, he'd call for me and say, "Miss, Kleiber, would you please peel the orange for me?"

It was always a navel orange that had no seeds. I'd peel it in one long stripe, the way my aunt Gertrude had taught me and arranged the sections on a porcelain plate. Because they looked like red-yellow half-moons and would rock back and forth, we called them *Reiterchen*—little rocking horse riders. When I finished, Mr. Sienholz said, "Thank you," and I went back to work. I think he liked looking at my hands—I had long, tapering fingers—but he never gave me a slice.

His wife came into the store from time to time, dressed to the nines. Mrs. Sienholz only shopped on the Kurfürstendam, where all the high-end stores were—Berlin's equivalent to New York City's Fifth Avenue—and she always wore one fur coat or another. Her favorite was a mink, with fur from head to toe, and a brown hat and brown shoes to match.

Sometimes, she brought along friends and acquaintances. She'd show them the newest leather products and schmooze and gossip until they felt compelled to buy something. She also liked to stand behind the cash register and ring up purchases for us.

She did give me one excellent piece of sales advice. "Costumers come in wanting to buy one of the pocketbooks they saw in the window," she said. "But we may no longer have it in stock. Your job is to make them feel that the ones we have on hand are as good or even better."

On one occasion, Mrs. Sienholz wore a dark-red fox stole. It was beautiful, cut so that the tiny legs and paws were at the collar and you could tie them at the neck or let them dangle. When she hung it on the coat rack stand in the stock room near the bathroom, I looked at it longingly. Finally, I took it and put it on. I was about to check myself out in the bathroom mirror when Mrs. Sienholz came in. I was so embarrassed I didn't say a thing, just took the coat off and hung it back on the coat rack. Later, I apologized to her, but she wasn't mad. So, I told her, "I just loved that coat," hoping she would give it to me, but she didn't.

Another time, she wore black suede shoes with straps around the ankle. When I saw them, I gushed, "Oh, Mrs. Sienholz, I like those shoes. They're so pretty."

Well, the next day she came in and gave them to me as a present. Lucky for me, they were my size and only slightly worn.

By then, I was sewing a lot of my dresses. But when it got cold and I needed a winter coat, I could not afford to buy one. Fortunately, Siemens had a company store where the employees could purchase clothes and shoes and pay for them over time. My parents took me there, and I picked out a winter coat. It cost 225 Marks, and I promised to contribute what money I could, but my father took care of it all.

On weekends, I'd go out with my friend Helga Kohlmeier. She was the daughter of our coal merchant. Her father never came home from the war, and she and her mother kept the business going. She was a year younger than me in school. After graduation, she worked in a factory. She had a nice figure and was warm and outgoing. We got along very well. Helga lived in the same apartment building as I, but around the corner in the Kösliner Strasse section on the fourth floor. We could see and talk to each other from our kitchen windows across the courtyard in back. Since we didn't have a telephone, we often communicated that way.

Sometimes she'd yell down to me, "Do you want to go to the movies?" I'd shout back, "Yes!" And that's what we did. We met up and went to the UFA movie theater in the Utrechter Strasse. It was within easy walking distance although we passed a lot of destroyed buildings along the way. So much had been ravaged during the war that it took a long time to clean all the rubble away.

At the theater, there was a small lobby with a ticket booth. The seating was divided into sections, and we always bought the least expensive seats in the first three rows. It meant leaning back and looking up at the big screen but we didn't mind. When the show started, we first watched a black and white newsreel about what had happened during the week, followed by a half-hour documentary about different places in the world. Then, the main feature started. Sometimes it was a German *Heimatfilm*, a romance in which the actors wore Dirndl dresses and Lederhosen. We also liked historical romantic dramas starring Ruth Leuwerik, O. W. Fischer, Romy Schneider, and Sonja Ziemann; war movies with Curd Jürgens and Hardy Krüger; and comedies with Liselotte Pulver and Heinz Rühmann. I especially liked *The Captain from Köpenick* because it was about Berlin during the 1880s and mocked the Prussian habit of taking orders without question from anyone dressed in a uniform.

I doubt that most people in the United States have heard of any of these actors and their films, but we sat in the dark theater enraptured. We also saw American movies—Westerns with Gary Cooper,

Glenn Ford, and John Wayne; Disney cartoons; and Alfred Hitchcock suspense thrillers.

By the time I was 16, I had a boyfriend. When my uncle Reinhardt courted his second wife, she had a son from her previous marriage, named Günther. We took a liking to each other. He was about six years older than me and worked for the Red Cross. Because he loved nature, we took walks in the woods, hand in hand, and he told me all about the trees and plants we passed. We didn't do any more than that—it was puppy love—which was a good thing because I found out that he was dating someone else at the same time.

My friend Helga had a bicycle, like me. One Sunday, we went for a ride and passed the house where Günther lived with his mother—she and my uncle had not yet married. She was talking with a neighbor outside, and when we stopped to say hello, she pulled me aside and said, "Trautchen, don't get too involved with my son. He is cheating on you."

I thanked her for telling me, and that was that. The next time I saw Günther, I didn't let on that I knew. I just said I wasn't ready for dating and we drifted apart.

After my brother finished *Volksschule*, he became a lifeguard for the Red Cross. In the summer, he worked at the *Plötzensee*, a small lake in Wedding with a public sand beach. The name *Plötze* means "roach" and refers to the fresh water fish that used to swim there.

One Saturday afternoon, Horst invited me to go swimming with him and two of his friends, and I decided to tag along. It was a sweltering hot day, and I spread out my blanket and lay down to bask in the sun. Suddenly, I felt myself being lifted up as Horst's friends took hold of the blanket, carried me to the edge of the water and threw me in the lake. I was so disoriented I didn't realize what was happening. Before I knew it, I was at the bottom, swallowing mouthfuls of water. I didn't know how to swim and panicked. I felt like I was drowning.

Fortunately, Horst saw me flailing, pulled me out, and gave me mouth to mouth resuscitation until I coughed up the water in my lungs. His friends couldn't apologize enough. They had wanted to play a joke on me and had no idea it would turn to near disaster. I didn't stay mad at them for long, but ever after, I became anxious around deep water, even in backyard swimming pools.

From time to time, salesmen stopped by at the shop to show new leather products to Mr. Sienholz. One of them drove a mint-green VW and hawked pocketbooks. He was blond-haired and blue-eyed and had a boyish look, although he was in his late twenties already. I liked him. He always stopped at my counter on his way out with something nice to say. But he was married. I could tell by the wedding ring on his right hand.

One day after work, he was waiting for me outside the store and said that he owned a Chow Chow that had just had a litter of three puppies, and he was trying to find a home for them. Would I like one of them?

I told him I had to first check with my parents since I was living at their apartment. That evening, when I mentioned it to my father, he said, "Ask him if he wants money. If yes, we're not interested. If no, why not?"

The next day, the salesman came back and I asked him. He said, "No, I just want to give you a dog." Then he continued, "You know, we can drive out to my parents and pick one out."

I was reluctant but decided to take a chance and got in the front seat. Being summertime, it was still light out. The half-hour ride took us into the outskirts of Berlin, and I started to get worried. But then we arrived at a house with a large garden. When we went inside, both of his parents were home, and I felt relieved.

The puppies were cute as buttons. One had a reddish color, another was silver-gray, and the third was a mix of black and white. I picked the red one, which looked like a miniature lion. Her name was Barlo. The salesman put a leash on her and handed it to me saying, "I know you're going to take good care of her." Then he drove me home, Barlo sitting in back of the car and me holding her leash from in front.

My father took to the dog right away. Barlo preferred men and, except for me, didn't like women or girls that much. My father trained her to take his lunch box into the kitchen in the morning, bring it to my mother, and drop it at her feet, so she could put in sandwiches before he went to work. He also trained her to go across the street by herself and do her business in the rubble. He would stand at the front entrance of our building every morning and evening and watched until she returned.

My mother wasn't as thrilled to have a new family member. There was no dog food in cans or bags available then. She had to go to the butcher, buy kidneys, cook them, chop them up, and let them cool on the window so that Barlo could eat them. "It's like taking care of a baby," she complained more than once.

But I was happy. On weekends, when I took the dog for a walk, I felt important. As I passed people, I thought, "Look at me. I have a Chow Chow!"

My brother liked Barlo, too. Horst was a stocky, muscular kid. When he held out his arm, Barlo jumped up, grabbed with her jaws, and held on while he paraded with her around the apartment.

At some point, my mother took Barlo to be bred—people paid a lot of money for purebred dogs. She asked the vet about it, and he set up an insemination with a black Chow Chow. Afterward, Barlo carried on like she was pregnant. Her belly started to swell up, and she no longer took the lunch box to my mother in the morning.

When it came time for Barlo to deliver, we made a bed for her and waited, but nothing happened. We stayed up through the night, and still nothing happened. The next morning, we were all exhausted, but

Barlo stood cheerfully in the kitchen with the lunch box in her mouth. All the swelling in her body had gone down and she looked perfectly normal. We were baffled. When my mother took her to a vet, he told us that Barlo had an imaginary pregnancy—it had been all in her mind.

We didn't tell may people about it because no one would have believed us. We had a hard time believing it ourselves. But the four of us were there and lived through it, so it did happen.

Meanwhile, it became clear that the salesman had not been generous out of the goodness of his heart. He had other designs on me. When he stopped by the shop now, he parked himself at my counter more deliberately. But I was still innocent and didn't know what he wanted.

When I told my mother, she said, "He wants you because when women get pregnant, they're not supposed to have sex anymore. I'm sure that's what he has in mind with you."

From that point on, I ignored him when he came into the store, or I disappeared into the stock room to dust off the pocketbooks. He soon got the message.

7

Owen

At some point, Mr. Sienholz decided to expand the business and open another store on Müller Strasse. By then, I was a trusted employee, and he asked Helga, an older salesgirl, and me to go there and run the shop. I was pleased that he and his wife gave me the opportunity. The store had square windows out front. Although it wasn't any bigger than the one on Badstrasse, it was more modern looking and brighter and more cheerful on the inside.

Mr. Sienholz and Mrs. Radomsky put Helga in charge of the cash register. Only she could ring up sales. I guess I wasn't that trusted after all, but I didn't mind. I rode my bicycle back and forth from home, parking it in the stock room in back during store hours.

The irony of the arrangement was that Helga ended up getting sacked for stealing from the till. Mr. Sienholz apparently kept scrupulous records and noticed a discrepancy between our inventory and sales receipts. It was a large enough sum for him to take measures. One afternoon, he and Mrs. Radomsky arrived in his Mercedes just as I left on my bike to ride home for the midday meal. When I returned, Helga was gone. Mr. Sienholz explained what had happened. He was almost apologetic, making sure I understood that I was in no way to blame. I felt sorry for Helga—she had always been friendly toward me and never put on airs—but I didn't let on, just nodded seriously. Mrs. Radomsky took over until they found a replacement for her.

Every two years or so, Mr. Sienholz bought a new Mercedes. He had it delivered to the old shop. Then, he loaded it up with leather goods and drove to our store. The first time, he came in and said to me, "Miss Kleiber, please go to the car and bring in the purses I left in back."

But when I stepped outside and looked around, I didn't see his black Mercedes anywhere. So, I went back, more mystified than embarrassed, and told him. He said, "Oh, yes, we had it painted. It's green now." He acted like it had slipped his mind. I could tell from the small, amused smile that played about his lips how pleased he was with his little joke.

Sure enough, there was a dark green Mercedes parked down the block, and it was brand-new. I unloaded the purses and didn't say anything more about it.

But two years later, the second time it happened, when I couldn't find the car, I said to myself, "I bet he got a new Mercedes." Looking around, I noticed a gray model with leather goods stacked on the back seat. When I returned to the store, my arms full of pocketbooks and purses, I said, "I see you had the car repainted again."

Mr. Sienholz stood there, with a perplexed expression on his face, not knowing what to say. I felt triumphant. Later, though, I worried that maybe I had gone too far, showing him up like that, but he said nothing more about it.

One day, as I was decorating the store window, a policeman passed by. He stopped and waited until I looked up. Then he waved and moved on. When I came out of the shop at the end of the day, he was standing there and offered to walk me home. He was dark-haired and good looking, and I liked his uniform. So, I said yes. But I didn't let him take me all the way to my house. When we got to Reineckendorfer Strasse, a block away from Weddingstrasse, I stopped at one of the buildings that was still standing and said, "Here we are." I went inside the front entrance and hid in the foyer until he was gone before walking the rest of the way home.

The next time he waited for me after work, I told him that I wasn't eighteen yet and not ready to have a relationship. Working late, often past regular hours, I didn't have the time to go out on dates. I don't know if he believed my explanation, but he accepted it. I noticed him a couple of times after that when I was in the window decorating, and he waved to me—it was his beat after all—but then he disappeared and I never saw him again.

I meet a cook the same way, decorating the window. He waited for me after closing time, too, and we talked for a while. He worked at the Hotel Graf, a fancy place, and he wore a stylish leather coat. He also walked me home, and I used the same ruse, ducking into a building until he was gone. When I arrived at the apartment, I told my parents about it, and they laughed because I had acted so smartly. My father said, "He'll probably be waiting for you every night and say, "It's not too far.'"

He was right. The following evening, there was the cook outside the store, eager with anticipation. I told him that I wasn't dating anyone, and took the hint. I did like the leather coat, though.

Our shop was on a busy commercial street, next door to a shoe store. One of the sales girls there, Irmtraut, and I became good friends. I had known her in *Volks-schule*, but we didn't talk much then because

Irmtraut and I.

she had been in the class ahead of me. Irmtraut had curly black hair and was shorter than me, but she had a lively, outgoing personality. Being a year older than me, she was considerably more experienced in the ways of the world.

One day, she asked me, "Do you want to go to the American Zone? Maybe we'll meet some Amis." Amis was slang for American soldiers. Living in the French sector, I hadn't encountered any, only seen them drive by in their Jeeps, because I had never set foot outside Wedding on my own. I felt a little daunted but said yes.

We rode the S-Bahn to the Lichterfelde district, where the American occupying forces were headquartered at the Andrew Barracks. During the Nazi period, the brick buildings—imposing, three- and four-story, sandstone edifices—had housed Hitler's personal SS guards. Now, the Americans had made them part of their compound.

We walked along the Hauptstrasse, which was a wide shopping street with a central divider, like the Badstrasse. At some point, we passed a leather goods store, and I stopped to look in the window to compare prices with ours. A Jeep slowed down and stopped at the curb. It was dark green and had a solid top. The two American soldiers inside were in uniform. One of them leaned out the window and called to us in English.

I looked at Irmtraut and she translated, "They want us to go with them."

Shaking my head, I said, "I'm not going."

She shrugged for their benefit, and they drove away. Before long, they were back, beckoning to us again. I barely glanced at them.

But when they came back a third time, I said to Irmtraut, "Let's hear what they have to say." I didn't speak a word of English and relied on her to translate. To my surprise, the one behind the wheel leaned over to the curbside window and said in German, "Hop in. We'll go for a beer."

Irmtraut giggled and poked me in the ribs. They seemed nice enough, so I said, "Okay."

I climbed in the back behind the driver, trying to act nonchalant. But I was so worried, I trembled all over. I could feel my teeth chatter.

The driver must have heard me because he turned around, put his finger on my chin, and said, "*Hab keine Angst*—Don't be afraid."

His touch sent a shiver down to my toes and drained all anxiety from me. I suddenly felt at ease. I would have gone anywhere with him.

He made the introductions: "I'm Owen and this is Carl." We gave our names, and to my surprise, he had no trouble pronouncing them. Then, we drove to an indoor beer garden where a band was playing. We sat at a table and each ordered a *Berliner Weisse*, a popular, local wheat beer. After we toasted each other, we danced and talked, with Owen and Irmtraut translating into German and English as needed.

As the evening wore on, I talked more with Owen. He understood German better than he spoke it, but we had no difficulty communicating. I told him a little lie, that I was eighteen, and mentioned where I worked.

Sergeant Owen.

He was twenty-four and a sergeant in the army—he pointed to the three stripes on his uniform so I would understand. He had joined the army on January 21, 1951 and was pleased that he ended up in Berlin because he had a German background. Although he didn't speak the language, he had picked up a lot and wanted to learn more. He had two brothers and two sisters and planned to go home the next year. The more he talked, the more I liked him. He came across so honest and sincere, and the way he looked at me made me feel all warm inside.

I was disappointed when Carl said they had to be at their barracks by midnight and it was time to leave. Lichterfelde was south of Templehof Airport and it would take them more than half an hour to drive us to the shoe and leather stores in Wedding and get back. On our way, there, I kept thinking, "Please, God, let him ask me out again."

When we arrived at the shops, Owen and Carl got out on either side and held the doors for us like real gentlemen. Owen took my hand as I climbed down. It was dark. The nearest streetlight was too far away for me to see his face. He didn't let go of my hand, though, and came closer. He said, "Goodnight," and then he kissed me, and I kissed him back.

Before he let go of my hand, he said, "I'm off on Sunday and I would like to see you again."

I said, "Me too."

And we made a date.

Then they drove away. I was so excited I nearly jumped for joy. I told Irmtraut, and she was happy for me even though she hadn't clicked with Carl. When she asked me if I wanted her to come along, just in case, I said, "No, I can manage on my own. I trust him."

Then I went home. I got there just before midnight, and my parents were up waiting, worried. I told them I had spent the evening at Irmtraut's house, and we'd gone out together. My mother knew her, so they relaxed and said it was okay. I hated to lie to them, but I couldn't tell them I'd been with an Ami. My father would have gone through the roof. Like many Germans who had fought in the war, he still considered Americans the enemy. The younger generation of German men didn't like them either because they had more money and often won the affections of the local girls. You could see "Ami Go Home" written on the walls of many a ruined building.

That Sunday afternoon, Owen and I met on Leopoldplatz, a small park with trees and a church at one end, not too far from my apartment building. I got there at the appointed time and looked for him. When I saw his Jeep, my heart started to beat faster. He got out and waved to me. He had changed from his uniform into slacks and a regular shirt. I wore beige pants and a blue and white striped blouse. We could have passed for any young, German couple out for the afternoon.

Although early fall, it was a warm day and we drove to the Berlin Zoo and walked around. The first time we saw another couple coming our way, Owen said, "Don't talk to me until we're past them. I don't want people to know I'm an American."

He was trying to avoid trouble. One time, when he was in uniform, we went to the botanical gardens. Owen brought his Voigtlander camera along. To get a better picture of me, he backed up onto the lawn. Immediately, a groundskeeper rushed over and yelled at him to stay off the grass. I'm sure if Owen hadn't been wearing an American army uniform, the man wouldn't have been so overbearing and nasty.

German girls who went with American soldiers didn't fare much better. Dating an Ami put you on the lowest rung of the social ladder. People called you *eine Nutte*—a slut—and worse. Much of the fraternizing going on was young people just having a good time, but in some cases, it led to children being born out of wedlock. What really irked the locals was to see interracial, married couples and black children in the strollers. In many ways, Germans were as racist as a lot of Americans—remember, in many U.S. states, interracial marriage was still illegal at the time!

So, I had to be careful and hide my growing relationship with Owen. Sometimes, he picked me up after work, away from the leather shop, and Irmtraut covered for me with my parents. We'd go out to drink beer and go dancing. Owen was a good dancer and held his own during the waltzes and polkas, but he came alive with swing numbers by Glenn Miller and Benny Goodman. I liked the slow dances most of all, when he held me tight.

Owen and me in front of his Jeep.

On weekends I took the S-Bahn and bus to Lichterfelde. From there, we explored other parts of Berlin in the American Zone—Kreuzberg, Steglitz, Zehlendorf. When the weather was warm, we went to parks, museums, and other tourist attractions. Sometimes, we visited the army headquarters, whose compound had a PX store and movie theater. We also spent time with one of Owen's army buddies, Barney, and his German girlfriend, Ruth. She was a translator at the American headquarters—she spoke English and French fluently—and they were planning to get married. Ruth was three years my senior and took me under her wing like an older sister.

Many of the movies we saw were in bright color, unlike the dreary, black and white German movies. Although they were in English, I could follow the story most of the time. I remember Gene Kelly in *An American in Paris* and Frank Sinatra in *On the Town*. All those skyscrapers gave me an idea of what New York City looked like. I liked

Westerns, too, because of the wide, open landscapes. I imagined that the rest of America looked like that. One time, we saw a cowboy film starring Audie Murphy, and Barney said, "That's my cousin!" When I looked at him in disbelief, he nodded vigorously. After the movie, he insisted that it was true, and I believed him. There was no reason for him to lie. He explained that Audie Murphy had fought in Italy and France and earned a lot of medals for his courage. As one of the most decorated soldiers of World War II, he'd had an easy in to Hollywood and made a successful movie career for himself. Barnie was very proud of him.

Ruth and Barney.

I managed to keep my relationship with Owen a secret for about eight weeks. Then I got caught. My mother had gotten suspicious and sent my brother to spy on me. When Horst followed me, he saw me walking arm in arm with Owen and ratted me out.

That night when I came home late, tiptoeing and quietly hanging up my coat, my father got out of bed. He had been waiting for me, and he was furious. I had never seen him so angry. He started to yell and slap me. Slamming the lower door from the wall cabinet against my leg, he drew blood. My mother joined in, shouting that I was a bad girl, a terrible disappointment to the family, and on and on. I let them rant without defending myself. After all, I had lied to them.

When they finally calmed down, I went to the kitchen, washed off the blood and put on a bandage. Then I went to bed, ignoring my parents and Horst, who had watched the uproar without saying a word. Before I went to sleep, I decided to leave home the next day.

In the morning, I got dressed and took the S-Bahn to Lichterfelde. At the barracks' entrance gate, I asked for Sergeant Owen Stanton. It took a while for him to come out. As soon as I saw him, I burst into tears. He took me in his arms until I got hold of myself. Then we went to a restaurant and I told him what had happened.

He said, "I'm going to see your parents and explain things. But in the meantime, I don't want you to go back. I can get a room for us, and you can stay there."

Lichterfelde had a middle-class section where large, three-story houses lined the streets. Many of the owners rented rooms to American soldiers. Some were war widows who had fallen on hard times and were happy to make a little extra money that way. We knocked on the doors of several houses until we found one where the woman who greeted us said, "Yes, I have a room and you can have it."

Owen went to buy some snacks and drinks for me at the PX. After he brought them to me, he left again, and I waited for him. The room was large and had pale green walls. It contained two beds, a dresser, and two armchairs. The woman was in her forties and had a kind face. She made me a cup of tea, and kept me company, listening to my tale of woe with sympathy. Then, she told me about her husband who had died of cancer just a year earlier. I felt safe with her.

The window looked out on the street, so I could see Owen driving up in his Jeep when his shift was over. He came dressed in civilian clothes and carried a bagful of presents with him—real coffee beans, chocolate, and cigarettes; and for me, a pair of nylon stockings to make me feel better. It worked, but I wasn't looking forward to facing my parents, even with him by my side.

We drove to Weddingstrasse, and Owen parked his Jeep in an empty spot in the ruins across the street, hidden from sight. My parents had been worried and were surprised when they saw him with me. They accepted his gifts stone-faced. Then, we all sat around the living room table. There was an awkward silence until Owen took out a cigarette. To everyone's surprise, Barlo, my Chow Chow, came over to him and licked his hand.

Then, Owen addressed my father and mother while I sat there quiet as a mouse. He spoke slowly and deliberately and said that he had good intentions and wanted to marry me. Because he was not re-enlisting, the army would not let him do that in Germany. His tour would be finished the following year, and I would have to come to America. Then he asked my father for my hand.

My father looked at him for a long time before getting up and shaking his hand. I rose, too, and threw my arms around my father. It meant so much that he accepted Owen. We were all relieved, and my mother brought beer for the two men. We kept on talking about what it was like outside of New York City on Long Island, where Owen's family lived, and what it would mean for me to join him in the United States.

I suppose my father forgave Owen for being an Ami because my mother had started to mention how good the Allies had been to us, bringing us food during the airlift. Unlike the Soviets in the Russian Zone, the Americans treated us with respect. Besides, the war was over, and he was home now. It was time to leave the past behind.

Soon, Owen became like a regular member of our family. He kept bringing us things from the PX that were hard for Germans to come by, much less able to afford. He would even cook in our kitchen. One time, he came with a chicken, and my mother didn't know how to prepare it. When Germans ate meat at home, they had schnitzel, goulash or sauerbraten, and on special occasions, duck or goose. So, Owen rolled up his shirt sleeves and roasted the chicken in our stove. Everyone agreed that it tasted finger-licking good.

He enjoyed being part of a German family. He fit in well and came whenever he had a free weekend. He spent Christmas at our apartment, and when spring came, he joined us at our garden cottage. Owen loved my parents and they grew to love him. My mother adored him. Some years later, she said to me, "Owen is such a handsome man. If I had been younger and in your shoes, I would have married him myself."

Owen and me in Lichterfelde.

We kept the room in Lichterfelde for our private use, although I always went home and never spent the night. I imagine my parents knew what was going on, but they never asked me about it. We took precautions and after the first time, I always enjoyed making love. I have never been ashamed to say that. Besides, I don't think Owen would have married me if we hadn't t made sure we were compatible that way.

One time, as we were lying in bed together, he said, "You know what I liked about you the first time I saw you? I looked you over, and I liked that you have big hips!"

It sounded odd to me, but I decided to take it as a compliment.

8

Leave Taking

Early in the summer of 1953, someone from our store told the boss I was dating an Ami. One of the girls I worked with and I had become friendly—she had a boyfriend much order than her, who was gray at the temples and took her to Spain and Italy on vacations. I opened up to her a little and told her I was with Owen. I doubt that she let the cat out of the bag intentionally, but she might have said something without realizing it. I don't think she meant to hurt me.

When I got off my bicycle at the store one morning, I was surprised to see Mr. Sienholz there. He told me he had been waiting for me and got down to business right away. "Miss Kleiber, I understand that you got into Jeep with an American soldier," he said.

I refused to lie and said, "Yes, his name is Owen Stanton. He is leaving in September, and I'll be following him to America to marry him."

He gave me a withering look that transformed into disappointment and regret, and said, "Well, we don't want anybody working here who is dating a former enemy of Germany. I'm sorry, but I have to let you go. Collect your things."

I was shocked and could feel my knees give way, but I caught myself and acted as if nothing was the matter. I wasn't going to give him the satisfaction to see me break down in tears. I took off my brown smock, collected my few belongings, and got my bicycle from the store room. The other salesgirls looked away, as if they didn't know me. On the way out, Mr. Sienholz stopped me and handed me the money I was due for the time I had worked that month. I took it and left with as much dignity as I could muster. But I cried on the way home.

In fact, I was devastated, but Owen and my parents made light of it. "Don't worry," they said. You'll get another job."

They were right. After a day or two of moping, I went to the unemployment office. It took only a little while before they sent me to another leather goods store, also in the French Zone. I had a good interviewed with the boss, a pleasant, middle-aged woman, got the job, and became a salesclerk again.

Meanwhile, Barney and Ruth got married, and Owen and I attended their wedding. It took place in a Protestant church in Lichterfelde, A lot of soldiers from the base came, looking spiffy in their uniforms. Barney wore his sergeant's dress uniform and Ruth had on a white fur coat. She was a pretty, dark-haired girl and looked great in it. Afterward, we had a party at her apartment. It was small place and everyone crowded into the living room. There was plenty of beer and music from the radio, and we all had a good time.

If Owen had reenlisted for another two years, we could have gotten married in Germany, too. He tried to make it happen anyway, but the military wouldn't allow it. They figured it was just a ploy for me to get to the United States. Owen might have considered reenlisting for my sake, but his brother had started a plumbing and heating business on Long Island, and Owen had promised to join him as soon as his tour of duty was up.

He left for the United States in September of 1953. The night before, we had a party with Barney and Ruth and drank rum and Coke. Boy, did I have a hangover the next morning. I was still feeling tipsy when I went to the train station to see Owen off—he was going to Frankfurt and from there by plane back to New York. We sat on a bench and held hands and talked about our future together. When he left the army, Owen would put all the money he'd earned into a bank account, so he could sponsor me. You needed someone financially stable to vouch for you, as well as a place to live. After going into business with his younger brother, Owen promised to arrange everything at his end and send me a plane ticket. I would have to apply for a passport, go to the American consulate for an emigration visa, and make sure I had all the necessary shots for small pox, typhus, and polio.

Saying good-bye to Owen at the train station.

When the train came, we embraced for a long time. Then Owen kissed me, hard and passionately, and went aboard. He kept talking to me from the window of his compartment until the conductor blew his whistle. Then, we touched hands, and the train started to pull away. I followed on the platform for a while and waved after him, feeling like there was an empty hole in my chest, but also hopeful for the future.

As a newlywed, Barney got permission to move into an apartment of his own near the barracks. It was roomier than Ruth's. I visited them for Sunday afternoon coffee as often as I could. Sometimes I brought a letter from Owen, and Ruth translated it for me into German. She also translated my letters to him into English and typed them up for me.

In the meantime, I kept working at the leather goods store. Because it was located in the French sector of Berlin, but closer to the barracks, we had a lot of soldiers as customers. At the beginning of the month, when they got paid, they came into the store in droves, wearing their yellow-brown dress uniforms with dark belts and military caps or berets.

Some of them tried to put their hands on my hips and behind, and when I slapped their fingers away, they just laughed. They smelled bad, too, like they walked with a cloud of sweat and garlic around them. I liked garlic but not in that quantity.

Some of them were sneaky and stole things. One time, three had me show them wallets and purses. I placed several on the counter in front of them. Glancing around the store, one soldier pointed to the top of one of the shelves and said, "Oh, I like that suitcase there. Would you take it down so I can have a closer look?"

I got a stepladder and pulled it off the shelf. He made a show of examining it closely but didn't end up buying it. Soon after, he and his companions left. As I put the wallets and purses away, I counted only six, not seven, and realized that one was missing. The soldier had just pretended interest in the suitcase to distract me while one of his companions slipped a wallet into his pocket. They had tricked me. I was mortified when I told my boss. I was afraid I would have to pay for it or worse, get fired again, but she reassured me. "It has happened before."

"But I feel so awful that they didn't buy anything,"

"I understand. I don't like it either," she said matter-of-factly. "But they are occupation troops, and we can't do anything about it. It's part of doing business with them. Just be more careful next time."

After that, I watched the French soldiers that came in like a hawk. I worked there for another month but grew tired of them being rude and trying to grope me. So, I told my boss I wanted to quit. She was very nice about it and "fired" me so I could collect unemployment again.

One afternoon in November, as I was walking home from the unemployment office on Badstrasse, I passed the leather goods store across the street. Mrs. Radomsky and Mrs. Sienholz were standing outside looking at the display window. They must have seen my reflection in the glass because they turned around they called out, "Miss Kleiber! Miss Kleiber!"

I stopped and they gestured for me to come closer. When I crossed the street, they asked, "What are you doing now? Are you working?"

I replied, "No. I'm getting all my papers in order. I'll be going to the United States in the spring."

They looked at each other. Then Mrs. Sienholz said, "We need help for the Christmas season. Do you want to work here until you leave?"

I didn't hesitate and said yes. There was no point carrying a grudge for the way they had treated me. I found out a little later that they replaced me with a friend of Mrs. Sienholz, and she proved to be a big disappointment.

I went to work in the old store, happy to earn money again. All the people who came in and knew me said hello, even if I wasn't serving them. The funny thing was that when the boss and his wife were there and an acquaintance of theirs entered the shop, they would always called on me, "Miss Kleiber, please come over here." Then they would turn to their friend and say, "Imagine, our Waltraut is going to emigrate to America. She met an American soldier and will fly to New York this spring to get married!" I had become an important person in their universe, someone they could show off.

Owen and I kept exchanging postcards and letters. For Christmas, he sent me a green suit with hearts made of pearls on the lapels.

The idea of going to America still felt unreal to me, until the airline ticket from Owen arrived in the mail. Now the date of my departure was set: March 22, 1954. From then on, time dragged along. At work, I went through the motions in an almost dream-like state. I didn't care about any of the Sienholzes' concerns. My heart was no longer in it.

In early March, my father, with German efficiency, made a to-do list for me—things I needed to accomplish before I left and things

I had to do once I got to the United States. Since my parents had no telephone in their apartment, I wouldn't be able to call them to let them know I had arrived safely. I had to promise to send them a telegram right away.

I asked him to take me to our garden cottage, so I could say good-bye to my grandparents and have a last look around to etch it in my memory. It was cold outside and I shivered because I no longer had the winter coat I got at Siemens—I had accidentally singed it on the burning-hot, metal door of the stove one day, and the damage could not be repaired.

There were so many people I wanted to say good-bye to, including the Koehns upstairs and the Sawadas in the deli below; the Kohlmeiers across the street and Irmtraut in the shoe store. They all wished me good luck and said, "Don't forget us."

I would have liked to visit all my relatives in East Berlin, but I was afraid to go, worried that the authorities there would keep me and prevent me from going to America. It was an irrational fear, of course, but I didn't want anything to jinx my departure.

Two weeks before I left, I visited Barney and Ruth for the last time. We went to a bar and had a beer. They promised to visit Owen and me when Barney's tour was up and he and Ruth came to the United States, too.

After that came good-byes with friends and neighbors and a big, final get-together with my grandparents, aunts, uncles, and cousins.

I quit working at the leather goods shop three days before my flight. My last evening there before store closing, Mrs. Sienholz came by, and she and her husband gave me a big, tan leather suitcase, a brass alarm clock, and a red leather travel kit as going away presents (I still have the travel kit). I took off my smock for the last time and handed it to Mrs. Radomsky. She and the other girls wished me good luck and hugged me. I was touched that they all cared so much for me.

My parents had another suitcase at home, and I packed as many clothes as I could, at least one outfit for every season. When they weighed it at the airport counter, it came to 40 pounds, but they took it without batting an eye. The airlines didn't charge for extra weight then the way they do now.

The morning of the flight, I said good-bye to Barlo, my Chow Chow. She wagged her tail as I petted her, not realizing she would not see me again. I was sad but felt that I was leaving a little bit of me behind for my parents because I had brought the dog into their lives.

When it came time for me to go, Mr. Sienholz was kind enough to drive my parents, Horst and me to the airport.

It was difficult saying good-bye to everyone. My father was trembling with emotion. He gathered himself long enough to say, "You are in good hands with Owen. I am so proud of you."

We embraced for a long time. Tears filled my eyes. I hugged my mother and Horst, too. Then, I walked to the gate where they checked my passport and exit visa. I sat in a waiting lounge with the other passengers for a while. When it came time to board the Pan Am flight, we all filed outside and walked on the tarmac to the waiting airplane. A tall metal staircase butted up to the front entrance. At the top, I looked back to the main building. I imagined my parents standing at the large picture window watching and waved even though I couldn't see them.

I don't remember the take-off or much of the flight, except that we had to stop in Greenland because the aircraft, a propeller plane, had a mechanical problem. We had to wait in a hanger. There were no chairs, and it was freezing cold inside. We stood around and sat on our suitcases. The crew didn't provide any food for us, not even a cup of coffee.

After what felt like forever, we finally got the go-ahead and boarded the plane again to continue our flight to New York.

9

Arrival

I came to the United States on March 22, 1954. Because of our unexpected layover in Greenland, the plane arrived late at New York's Idlewild Airport. It's called Kennedy Airport now. Going through customs took a while because in those days, the American officials checked just about every piece of luggage. There were make-shift tables in a large hall, and we had to open up our suitcases while the inspectors rifled through our clothes. They were worried about people smuggling plants and agricultural products into the Unites States and confiscated any non-processed food items.

By the time, I made it through unscathed, I was worried that no one would be there to pick me up. But when I stepped outside the Pan Am terminal, there was Owen waiting for me, standing next to a mint green Chevrolet convertible and grinning from ear to ear. He was wearing tan slacks and a gold colored corduroy shirt with a pattern of little black squares. I rushed into his arms and we smothered each other with kisses.

He put my suitcases in the back seat—the interior of the car was plaid—and drove to his parent's house in Huntington, Long Island. It was a warm day and he kept the top down. I was beginning to shake, all the tension of the trip draining from my body. By the time we got there an hour and a half later, I was feeling okay again, ready for the welcoming committee.

When we pulled into the driveway on Bennett Avenue, the first to come outside to greet us were Owen's sisters, Junie and Marie, gawking at the stranger from Germany. Junie was three years older than me with medium-brown hair. Marie was only 15, but she was very pretty and looked quite mature for her age. Then came Owen's parents and his ten-year-old brother Billy. His father, Owen Christopher (my Owen's second name was George), was a tall man with gray, thinning hair and Swedish-Norwegian features. He smiled and I liked him right away. In contrast, Owen's mother, Viola, was a small, petite woman with dark brown hair and brown eyes. Her evaluating glance put me a little on edge. All I could say was "Hello"—I still didn't speak any English—and Owen did his best to act as translator.

They invited me inside into a suburban living room with a table, sofa, chairs and a TV set in one corner. I was glad that they had prepared some cold cuts. I was ravenous after the long trip and happy to be eating so I didn't have to talk.

The house was a two-story summer cottage, a bungalow that belonged Owen's uncle, who rented it to my in-laws. It had a living room and kitchen on the first floor and two bedrooms upstairs. Owen slept on the couch downstairs. I slept with his two sisters in one bedroom, sharing a bed with Junie. Owen's parents shared the other room with Billy.

Owen was keen on getting married and moving into a place of our own right away. So, the next day, after sending a telegram to my parents in Germany as promised, we met with the minister at the Presbyterian church in town. Father Roth had a kind face. He wore a full-length dark robe over a white shirt and black tie and invited us into his office. When Owen explained our situation, he was helpful and friendly and had us sign various forms. The earliest date on his calendar for the wedding ceremony was Saturday, April 3, and we eagerly agreed.

That gave us only two weeks, and there was a lot to get done. I had no idea what was required to get ready. Fortunately, we met Owen's brother Harold and his wife Muriel that afternoon, and they promised to help us. Moo—everybody called her that—was petite and pretty. She took me to a store and bought curtain fabric—white with little velvet rosebuds. She picked out a pattern and made me a wedding dress. It had long sleeves and a high neckline with buttons all the way down to the waist. While Moo sewed, I made myself useful by covering all the buttons with fabric.

My mother-in-law pitched in, too. Whenever I asked Owen what they were doing, he said, "Oh, don't worry about it. They have everything under control."

We went apartment hunting and found a place we could afford. It was a cold-water flat with a separate entrance on the second floor of a private house on Fairmont Street, near the Huntington Rural Cemetery. We bought furniture—bedroom, living room and kitchen sets— as well as pots, pans, dishes and silverware to outfit the place. I liked the bedroom set most of all. We took it with us whenever we moved to another house.

The night before the we got married, I set my hair in curlers. I was so excited I could hardly sleep. In the morning, Moo helped me get dressed and we were off to church. Only members of the immediate family attended. The men all wore their best suits, and the women their Sunday dresses. My father-in-law walked me down the aisle. Moo acted as my maid of honor, and Harold was Owen's best man. The actual ceremony was mercifully brief. Not knowing the language made it difficult for me to follow, but I managed to say "I do" at the right moment. Afterward, everyone gave me a hug and kissed me on the cheeks. I guess they all said something nice, but I didn't understand any of it and replied only "Yes" and "Thank you."

I was happy to receive a congratulatory telegram from my parents who said they wished they could have been here.

We had a small party at the house. There was potato salad and beer, and Owen's mother had baked a wedding cake. I had chipped one of my front teeth in Germany and it hurt when I had food or drinks that were too hot or cold, so Harold warmed up the beer for me. Compared to what I was used to in Berlin, it tasted like water. You could drink all you want and not feel any effects.

Owen and I at the wedding reception.
His brother Billy on the far right.

Owen and I left the party and drove to our apartment. His siblings had tied a bunch of tin cans to the back of the Chevy, and they made a lot of noise dragging behind. Our wedding night was lovely, although it took forever to get my dress off because it had all those buttons down the front and on the sleeves, too. Fumbling with them, Owen fumed, "Did you have to have so many buttons?" but he finally managed and declared victory over the dress. After that, we had fun.

It was still cold in April, and our apartment was quite chilly, so we bought a kerosene heater. The electric kitchen stove was made of cast iron. To do the laundry, I had to heat up water in pots, dump it into the bathtub—an old-fashioned, free-standing tub with four legs. Then, I put down a towel on the floor, got on my knees, and used a washboard to scrub pants, shirts, socks, and underwear clean. I'd hang them in the attic to dry, just like in Germany. But I couldn't do the bed sheets that way, so I took them to a laundromat.

After Owen went to work in the morning with his brother, I would listen to soap operas on the radio. One was *Our Gal Sunday* about an orphan girl from a Colorado mining town who marries a British aristocrat. I started to learn English by repeating the words I heard. I also got books and magazines and associated words and the pictures. I didn't have a dictionary, so I'd write down words I didn't understand, and at night Owen would tell me what they meant. He could follow my broken English pretty well and corrected my pronunciation and grammar. Sometimes, to make it easier for me, he would talk to me in German.

Owen and Harold were working hard to get their business, "Suburban Plumbing and Heating," off the ground They'd bought a truck and

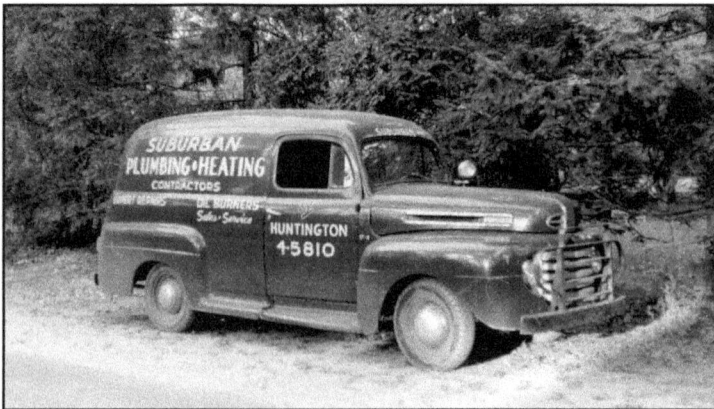

Owen and Harold's truck.

tools and went around repairing oil burners and installing new heating systems. They put in new dishwashers, faucets, and bathtubs into older homes and some of the new houses that were being built as the suburbs started to expand in the 1950s. I don't know how they learned to do all that stuff. Like my father, Owen was good with his hands and could pick up just about any trade quickly.

Shortly after we moved into the apartment, I became pregnant. Owen reminded me that with my big hips, I should have an easy time giving birth. But it didn't turn out that way. I was in labor for considerable time before our son David was born on May 12, 1955 at Huntington Hospital.

Owen, baby Dave and I in my in-law's backyard.

Dave was a good baby and slept at night, but it was hard being alone with him at home all day. I had made a lot of baby clothes for him already on a sewing machine Owen bought me, and I knew how to change his diapers, feed him, and rock him to sleep. But I felt isolated and didn't have anybody to keep me company. Sometimes, I called my mother-in-law on the telephone, but I couldn't speak English very well yet and had a hard time making myself understood. So, I had to wait until Owen came home.

Now that I had to deal with diapers, the hardest thing was doing the laundry, because the kerosene stove didn't heat enough water. I had to do several loads, which took me forever, but I managed somehow.

Things got better when I got a stroller. I'd bundle Dave up in it and go to the bus stop at the corner of our street. Getting the stroller onto the bus was always a struggle, but people were kind and helped me. We rode to downtown Huntington and I shopped at Grants and bought groceries at the A&P. Then, I loaded them into the stroller with Dave and brought them back home. Gradually, as Dave got older and we settled into a routine, I got to know my in-laws better. Because we didn't have a television, we went to Owen's parents' house—they had a big dark wood DuMont TV console—and watched *I Love Lucy, Ozzie and Harriet, Dragnet, Davy Crockett*, and the *Ed Sullivan Show*.

Junie was always friendly to me. She was married, but her husband was no longer in the picture. He had taken off one day and never returned, so she was stranded for the time being. She worked at Grant's Department store in town. Later, after her divorce became official, she married a sweet, sensible man named Bill. They never had kids, but loved their black poodle, and she always remembered the birthdays of my two children and sent them cards with money in them.

Marie was a little princess who liked to wear pretty clothes and tight-fitting jeans and tops. She usually bought them a size too small to show off her figure. Every week she needed a new dress. When Owen was still in the Army in Germany, he had sent money to help his parents out. But after he came home, he found out that Marie had spent it on clothes rather than food for the family, and he blew his stack. Not that he could do anything about it. In the eyes of her mother, Marie could do no wrong.

She liked to go dancing and often came home at night with runs in her stockings and her dress torn at the seams because it was too tight for her. Her father bought a sewing machine to fix them, but no one in the family besides Moo could sew, and I ended up mending her clothes when we came over.

Sometime later, Marie married a man named Frank, who worked for the township's government. They got along well and had two boys, and a girl. After they moved to Florida, we saw them only occasionally when they came back for a visit.

Billy was just boy when I arrived. He didn't give anybody any trouble. He went to school, lived at home, and kept to himself. When he grew up, he got married and lived on a houseboat in Oyster Bay for a while with his wife and their daughter. At some point, they moved to Florida, too, and we lost contact with them.

I liked Owen's father. He had an outgoing personality, smiled a lot, and was always good to me. If someone needed anything, he would help at the drop of a hat. He drove a van and made deliveries, first for a department store, and later for a furniture store. Billy and Marie's husband Frank helped him with the heavy lifting. He liked being surrounded by his family and often mentioned that his biggest dream was to live on the top of a mountain with his five children's homes below in the foothills, but that never came to pass.

My mother-in-law, Viola, was another matter. She was the same age as my mother and looked younger than her forty-eight years. She had a great figure—you'd never have thought that she had borne five children. When she told me early on she was of French and German descent, I had high hopes that she would become like a mother to me. But she was stand-offish, and I soon realized that she didn't like me. She was disappointed that Owen hadn't married an American girl and often made her views quite clear.

Apparently, he had dated a girl named Gloria for a while—I never met her—and Viola had liked her. She would criticize me by saying things like, "Oh, Gloria would have done this," and "Gloria would have done it like that."

One day, I finally had it and told her, "*You* should have married Gloria!"

One afternoon, Viola, Moo and I went to Korvette, a discount store, and I bought a black, corduroy jumper and a red blouse. At that point, we were living next door to each other, and when Owen came home, he and his mother talked over the fence out back.

Later, during dinner, he said, "Why don't you show me what you bought today."

I asked, "How do you know?"

"Mama told me you all went shopping."

So, I brought the clothes out, and showed him the price tags which I hadn't cut off yet. The one for the blouse was $1.99; the one for the jumper, $4.99.

When he glanced at me with an odd expression, I asked, "What's going on? Why are you looking at the tags?""

He looked a bit sheepish and said, "Because Mama told me they cost $7.99 and $11.99."

Viola knew exactly what they had cost, but she wanted to convince him that I spent money frivolously. The nerve of that woman! I was going to give her a piece of my mind, but Owen said to let it go.

From that point on, I always left the tags on in case he wanted to check them, but he never did. He believed me when I told him the price of the things I bought.

Owen had two aunts, his mother's sisters. One of them had died of brain cancer before I arrived. The other, Harriet, had a good job with the Topps Chewing Gum Company, which invented selling bubble gum with baseball cards. She lived in an apartment in Brooklyn. A beautiful woman, she always dressed elegantly. When Owen was younger, he spent time at her place whenever taking care of five kids became too much for his mother—he was Aunt Harriet's favorite nephew. When she came to visit us, she always brought clothes for my children, first Dave and later, Shirley. She was a good soul.

I thought Harold and Moo were the perfect couple. Although nineteen months younger than my husband, Harold was taller than him. He was a good-looking guy, light brown hair, and not a bit of fat on him. Moo seemed to have boundless energy, raising her children, taking them shopping with her, always on the go. Sometimes she picked them up and we went shopping together. She always stood up for me.

One time, I made new curtains for the kitchen and a matching table cloth, the way my mother had done in Berlin. When my mother in-law-came by, she said, "Did you make those curtain?"

I said, "I did."

Then, she noticed the table cloth and commented, "Why are you putting a table cloth on the kitchen table? You don't see me doing that. It's too much work."

The next time I saw Moo, I told her what had happened, and she said, "Don't take Viola seriously, Wally. That's how she is. She acts that way with me. Now she has two people to complain about." Then she laughed and gave me a hug. Moo had a good sense of humor. I liked her a lot.

By then, I had changed my first name. Much as people tried, most of them could not wrap their tongue around "Waltraut" without mispronouncing it. In those days, everybody's name got shortened —Robert to Rob, William to Bill, Muriel to Moo—so when Owen's father called me Wally, it stuck. At first, it sounded odd to me, but I soon grew to like it!

10
Long Island

Meanwhile, Owen and Harold continued to expand their business. At some point, their lawyer suggested that they start building houses and cash in on the postwar construction boom. So, they bought property, put up homes and sold them. Their architect referred them to his clients, and they ended up building their houses, too.

The first project, though, was a ranch home for Harold and Moo. By then, they had three children, Harold Jr., Gary, and Janet (a fourth, April, was yet to come), and their apartment was getting too crowded. They needed more space. That was the first house Owen and Harold built together, a stand-alone in the Westville area of Huntington near Walt Whitman High School.

One day, Owen came home all excited and announced. "I bought a big piece of property. I'm going to build a house for us."

I said, "I don't want a house. I want a nice apartment. What am I going to do with a house?"

"Well, don't you want a house like my brother has?"

I was still doing the laundry on a washboard in the bathtub and asked, "Can I have a washer and dryer?"

Owen said, "Yes, you can have it all."

"In that case, I'm all for it!"

So, he and Harold built us a ranch home with three bedrooms on Shady Lane in Greenlawn, just east of Huntington. The house had a full basement, a large living room, a kitchen with the most modern appliances, and a nice yard. Owen turned one of the three bedrooms into his office. Living there was a wonderful improvement over our cold-water flat.

*Our first house on Shady Lane, with Owen's work truck
and Dave standing next to our 1957 DeSoto.*

His efforts to teach me how to drive were less successful. We had a 1957 DeSoto Firesweep, and when I got my learner's permit, I drove it all the way home from the motor vehicle bureau. As we got to the house, Owen said, "Slow down," and I got so flustered that I couldn't find the brake petal. He put his hand down on it to stop the car. Flustered, I stepped hard, crushing his hand. He yelled bloody murder and yanked it away. In the process, he tore it on the corner of my shoe. When I saw it bleeding, I fled up the driveway into the house and locked myself in the bathroom until Owen came and talked to me. He laughed about what had happened, but that was the end of me trying to drive the De Soto.

That summer, Barney and Ruth came for a visit. They had settled in Texas and had a three-year-old son, Michael. We had a wonderful time reminiscing about Berlin and sharing our dreams for the future. I also learned a big lesson in how kids can influence one another. At the time, Dave was only two and not yet potty trained. But Michael took him to the bathroom, showed him the ropes, and by the time our friends left, my son knew what to do! Unfortunately, we did not keep in touch and never saw Barney and Ruth again. I have often wondered what happened to them.

When I became pregnant again, we planned for my parents to visit us so that my mother would help with the newborn baby. They were all ready to go, but when they got to the airport in Berlin, there was no plane. The charter airline that had sold them the tickets was a scam outfit and left them and the other passengers stranded. When I received their telegram, I was heart-broken.

My daughter, Shirley, was born on June 16, 1961. The year before, the Ames Brothers had released a song that became a big hit, "The Naughty Lady of Shady Lane." Naturally, everyone in the neighborhood called Shirley that when we took her out in her baby carriage.

Shirley was a little hellion. Before she was a year old, she would stand up in her crib and rattle the railing, demanding to be picked up. When she heard Dave and his friends play outside in the yard, she would rock and bounce her crib to the window so she could watch.

After we came home from the hospital, Owen tried to teach me to drive again. He bought a mini station wagon for me, a 1959 Ford Squire with a stick shift on the floor in a three-speed H pattern. He drew it on a piece of paper so I could visualize the way the gears worked and practice shifting on my own. I laid it under my pillow at night hoping it would magically seep into my mind while I was asleep, but it didn't help. I could never get that shifting pattern down. So I told Owen that I didn't like the stick shift at all, and he sold the car; and I gave up on trying to get my driver's license.

The following year, on February 2, 1962, I became a United States citizen. By then, my English had improved to the point that I could carry on extended conversations without having to search for words or come up with different expressions when I didn't know how to translate a German word that popped into my head.

The swearing in took place in Riverhead, Long Island. I put on my best dress and hat, and Owen drove me there and waited outside the office. I took my birth certificate, German passport, and entry visa with me.

An immigration officer dressed in a dark suit and tie ushered me into a small room. He was in his late 40s and very tall. I had to look up to him. There was an American flag in the corner next to a bank of filing cabinets and a desk. The man took the chair behind it and I sat across from him. He looked over my papers and nodded that they were okay, Then, he engaged me in conversation.

"How many children do you have?" he asked.

"Two," I said. "A boy and a girl."

"How do you spell that—two?"

"T-W-O."

Who is the governor of New York?"

I knew that. "Rockefeller."

"Do you know who the presidents is?"

"Eisenhower," I said without any hesitation.

He said, "Okay."

In retrospect, I think he just let it go. Of course, John F. Kennedy was President of the United States by then. I'd mixed them up. Perhaps he was impressed that I knew Eisenhower's name. He asked me a few other things—when I first came to America and if I lived on Long Island. Finally, he got up and told me to stand, too, raise my left hand, and say after him, "I hereby declare, on oath,… that I will support and defend the Constitution and laws of the United States of America against all enemies, foreign and domestic…"

And I did, word for word, all the way to "so help me God."

When I was done, he shook my hand and said, "Congratulations, you are now an American. We will send you your naturalization papers in the mail."

I said, "Thank you very much," and left.

As I walked out of the building into the chilly February afternoon, I felt elated and proud. When Owen and I got home, we celebrated. Even thought it was still early, we each had a shot of German brandy, Asbach Uralt—my favorite.

I could hardly wait for the document to arrive. When it did, Owen and I celebrated all over again.

Meanwhile, Owen and Harold embarked on their next big building project. They bought a large parcel of land on Spruce Drive, empty except for an older, attached, two-family house off to one side. After they fixed that up, Owen's parents moved in on one side, and Marie and Frank took the other. The brothers built five split-level houses on the remaining land. The model home was in the middle.

Our house on Spruce Drive with the "Model" sign still in the front yard.

Four of the new homes sold quickly, but no one wanted to buy the model because it came completely finished. At the time, people liked to fix up the basements of their new houses themselves, and this one had a playroom, bathroom, and small kitchen downstairs already. So, when Owen and Harold needed money to buy more land to build on, we purchased it for ourselves.

It had a beautiful kitchen, three bedrooms, and an office for my husband. After work, Owen entered through the garage and took a shower in the basement bathroom before coming upstairs.

Owen's parents living next door had its downsides and blessings. Having my mother-in-law looking over my shoulder became annoying, but I appreciated her pitching in to help with my children.

When Shirley was three years old and playing out in the backyard, a neighbor's dog bit her. She was chasing a ball that she had kicked. There were no fences between the two properties. A black terrier belonging to the Stenner family that lived two doors from us pursued the ball, too. As Shirley and he both went for it, he jumped up and bit her under her right eye. Screaming and crying, she ran to find me. Mrs. Stenner must have seen it happen because she came racing to our house, even though she was pregnant with her third child and quite far along. She drove us to a doctor who gave Shirley a tetanus shot and stitched up the wound.

When I returned home, Mr. Stenner came over and apologized. Then he said, "I want you to sue me. I have insurance that will pay." We ended up getting $2,000, which we put in a bank account for Shirley and, later on, she bought her first car with it. Everyone in the neighborhood put up fences after that, although the dog could easily have burrowed under or jumped over them if he'd wanted to. Shirley still has a small scar as a permanent souvenir, but the experience left no emotional marks, and she has had dogs of her own since.

Meanwhile, we had a lot of fun as a family. Music was important to Owen. We had a radio and a box record player, and listened to pop and country tunes—Elvis Presley, Patsy Cline, Rosemary Clooney, Dinah Shore. I loved the songs from musicals—*Oklahoma, Carousel, The King and I*. We'd see the movie, and when we bought the recording and played it later on, the songs would allow me to relive the movie all over again.

On the Fourth of July, Owen put on a record of John Philip Sousa tunes, and we marched around the house to celebrate. We'd start in the kitchen, head down the long hallway, go through the living and dining room, and end up back in the kitchen. Owen paraded in front, I followed behind him, and Dave and Shirley brought up the rear. It was a great way to celebrate, especially when the fireworks came on, and it became an annual tradition. In our house, there was no Fourth of July without Sousa.

Like many American families, we cherished our cars, and Owen introduced Dave early on to what became a life-long obsession for my son. One Saturday, he took him along to buy a new car. In the dealer's showroom, they saw a Studebaker Golden Hawk, black with red interior. In those days, the salesmen would put a plate on the car and let you drive it home to "show the missus," knowing that the buying decisions usually required her consent.

Soon, Owen and Dave arrived all excited in the Studebaker. Dave dashed into the house to get me to come check it out. I had to admit it looked very handsome sitting in our driveway, but on closer examination, I realized it wouldn't do.

"Its so small inside, Owen. Where are the kids going to sit?" I said.

"What do you mean?" he asked, genuinely mystified.

"There's not much room in back and the kids will grow so fast," I said. "No, I don't think so."

I hated to burst his bubble, but it couldn't be helped. Dave was disappointed, too. Fortunately, Owen respected my opinion and took the car back without complaint.

Later that afternoon, they returned with a Chrysler 300, red exterior and red leather seats. It was slightly used, having been driven by the wife of the owner of the dealership, but it had only a few hundred miles on it. There was more room in the back.

"That is more like it!" I exclaimed, and everybody in the family was happy.

Shirley and Dave in front of our Chrysler 300, Easter 1963

In the summer of 1964 my parents finally came to visit us for the first time. Like grandparents everywhere, they doted on my children who called them Oma and Opa. It had been a little more than ten years since I'd left Berlin, and I was so happy to see them. They had aged. Both had graying hair and were retired by then. My father had developed emphysema in one lung. Smoking all his life had caught up with him. There were times when he had difficulty breathing, but he kept his humor about it. He told us that the first time he'd had a severe attack, my mother had taken him to a doctor, who checked him out and prescribed a lot of medication. When my father asked, "How is my lung? Is it very bad?" the doctor nodded and said to him with German gallows humor, "I think you should throw it away."

113

One small benefit of his illness was that my parents had a telephone installed in their apartment, which made it easier for us to communicate.

We spend a lot of time catching up, and I found out what had happened to everyone I'd left behind in greater detail than what my father had told me in his letters, which he wrote on a typewriter. Although the Berlin Wall divided the city in half—the Russians had put it up in the summer of 1961 to stem the flow of East Germany's citizens to the West—my mother went into East Berlin every month to visit her sister and take along food and other presents. My aunt Gertrude and her children were doing the best they could.

My brother Horst had gotten married to a young woman named Ingrid and they had two children (later, they had two more). I was pleased for him even though my parents didn't seem very happy when they shared the news. I didn't pursue it then, but I learned later on that they had considerable difficulties with him after I left Germany and he grew older.

One evening, we put on a record and my mother and I waltzed together around the living room. She was a great dancer and, with her leading, it felt like we were floating on air.

It was wonderful to reconnect and spend time with the two people who meant so much to me. But I also realized how different our lives and attitudes had become. My parents were much more formal than their American counterparts. My father always put on a shirt and tie when he got up and wore them all day, even at night and on weekends when everyone else relaxed. My mother would get dressed up in the morning and put on ear rings like she was going to the theater or a concert. All that was missing were a pair of gloves.

When she saw Shirley playing on the patio, she came inside and said to me, "Don't let her sit there—she'll get all dirty." It had never occurred to me to discipline my children for playing outside. If they got dirty, they could take a shower or bath. In Germany, hot water was still at a premium and people bathed at most once a week.

Meanwhile, Owen and Harold continued to build custom houses with great success. On one large piece of land, they put in a road and constructed two-story, square-shaped residences with three bedrooms, kitchen, living room, dining room and garage. They were very reasonably priced, costing only $17,990.

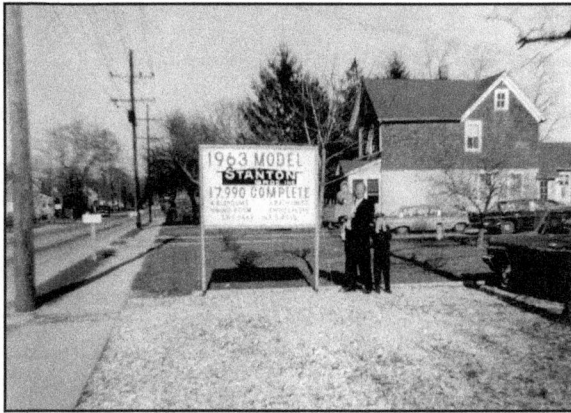

Owen with Shirley and Dave
on the parcel of land he and Harold developed.

In Greenlawn, east of Huntington, they put up two ranch houses near the Long Island Railroad. Each had a big basement and a large garden in back. They hand fitted stone facades in front, piece by piece. The homes looked impressive when they were finished.

Owen picked up a lot of skills pursuing the building trade. He became an expert plumber, electrician and carpenter. He bought all kinds of tools so that he would have the right one for the job at hand. If he needed one that didn't exist, he'd invent it. One time, when he didn't have a helper to hold the copper pipes he wanted to cut, he built a tripod with a clamp that gripped them so he could have both hands free and do it on his own. Being curious, I often watched him work. I learned a lot from him and have always felt comfortable fixing things around the house.

When Owen and Harold bought a good-sized parcel of land in East Northport for development, they put in a street and called it Owen Place. Then, they built a number of houses. One of the original owners still lives in her home there, and the street still carries Owen's name.

Owen Place circa 2019.

My husband was really a frustrated architect. He would have loved to go to school to get certified, but his parents didn't have the money. So, he did all the design work and drew the plans himself. Then, he had an architect put a seal on them and went to the county building department to get the necessary permits. Altogether, the Stanton brothers built close to 30 homes on Long Island. At times, they had as many as three other people working for them. Things were going well.

But Owen's working relationship with his younger brother didn't always run smoothly. Harold was not an easy person to get along with.

He could be arrogant and sarcastic. Sometimes, I heard him and Owen arguing and yelling in the office downstairs.

Maybe because my husband was older, Harold felt he needed to assert himself. But he did it in selfish ways. Although Owen did all the design work and drawings, Harold would often take the credit. Sometimes, with a client, he'd say, "I didn't care for the way Owen drew this, so I redid it." I overheard them because the client conferences took place in our living room, and it made me mad. I knew Herold never touched a pencil.

We got up early in the morning, and Owen had breakfast, went downstairs into his office and did administrative work. He drew up building plans and kept the books, paying bills, taxes and employees. But when he got to the construction site, Harold would say crudely, "You're late. Couldn't get out of bed because Wally wanted to get a little? Why can't you do that at night?" He always thought we were lazing around.

One time, I had enough and told him, "Harold, I'm going to bring over all the books and you can do them yourself. You make room in your house for the office because I don't want it here anymore."

He acted surprised, "What do you mean?"

I said. "Because you are nasty and have bad thoughts about us in your head all the time."

Owen ran interference and smoothed things over. Later he said to me, "Let it go. Let him say what he wants."

Another thing that irritated me was that Owen would spend most weekends at the spec houses in case people showed up to have a look. Harold never did that. He loved boating and took Moo and his four kids out on the water, happy that Owen was taking care of sales.

Ultimately, what ended their partnership, though, was that big home builders came to Long Island in the mid-1960s and bought up all the empty property. They put up 30 houses in a month, and there was no way the Stanton brothers could compete with that. Being a custom builder, Owen refused to cut corners to speed up the process.

So, he lost interest in the construction trade when he couldn't compete or build according to his perfectionist values. For a short while, he took a job with Sears in the plumbing department. Then he went to work for a carpenter. Owen got busy enough that he needed an assistant. On weekends, he often helped Harold who had taken up plumbing full-time again.

Owen also began to paint in his spare time. As with anything visual, he showed a remarkable aptitude. Some of his works hang on the walls of my home now.

Soon, something else started to occupy his mind. When he was a teenager, his father had bought a farm in upstate New York along with some cows and taken his wife and five children to live there. He'd kept working in the city and commuted on weekends.

For some reason, Owen remembered it as an idyllic time in his life, and he wanted to try it for himself. When he shared his dream with me, I was reluctant but supportive. I was a city girl. The closest I'd ever come to a cow was in Luckenwalde, but even there, it was from afar, when I watched herds graze on the meadows in the distance.

Still, I went along as we drove to upstate New York on the weekend to look at farms. I was secretly hoping that he would get it out of his system. But we came upon one Owen liked in Coxsackie, a town on the Hudson River 20 miles south of Albany. It was a 155-acre spread and he bought it. We sold our house in Long Island, packed up our belongings, and moved there in October of 1968.

11

Farm Girl

The farm was located on Flint Mine Road about two miles south-west of the town of Coxsackie. More than 12,000 years ago, Indian tribes lived there and mined the area for flint to make tools and weapons. If you walked in the nearby woods, you would find arrowheads on the ground. Owen and Dave took Shirley there and they always found some. Archaeologists digging in the cave on Flint Mine Hill, which we could see from our farm about a mile to the north, found caribou bones from animals the Paleo-Indians had hunted and eaten. In 1978, the Flint Mine Hill Archaeological District was placed on the National Register of Historic Places.

There were two residential buildings on and near our property in addition to a big barn, a silo, a small milk house, and a tool shed with plows, a manure spreader, and other farm equipment.

The barn, silo and tool shed on our farm.

One was an old farm house, where the previous owners, the Baldwins, lived until they found another residence. It was a bit run-down. The other, a two-story, red brick house with a large porch, was in better shape. Unfortunately, it also had people living in it and hadn't been part of the sale.

Shirley, Dave, a school friend and me in front of the old farm house.

Owen purchased 40 heifers right away. He was all ready to move into the old farm house and get going on his dairy farm adventure. I normally went along with him, but that time I put my foot down. I wasn't going to live in a ramshackle place with my two children. So we rented a mobile home twenty minutes away and lived there. In the morning, we piled into the car and drove to the farm to take care of the cows.

When the brick house became available, we bought it. But it required work, too. All the water pipes were calcified because the water in that region was so hard. The kitchen looked run down. All the countertops were covered with linoleum.

Since we had sold the house on Long Island, we had money to fix it up. Owen bought a dishwasher, dryer, and new kitchen cabinets. He replaced the refrigerator and hooked up the appliances but never got around to installing the cabinets. We were too busy. They sat in an empty room the whole time we lived there.

The brick house where we lived.

The cows needed to be milked twice a day. After I washed the heifers down from head to hooves, including their udders, Owen attached the suction devices to their teats from the milking equipment he'd bought. When he was done with one, he emptied the milk into a pail, and I carried it to the milk house, where I measured the volume and poured it into a holding tank. I wrote in a ledger which cow it was and how much milk she had given. Then, I rinsed the bucket and went back, repeating everything until we were done.

That happened at six in the morning. Afterward, I had to cook breakfast and put Dave and Shirley on the school bus. I had to wash all the milking machines every day with lye and clean the barn. When inspectors came, they put on white cotton gloves to check if there was any dust. The storage equipment had to be spotless, too, and the milk had to have a certain fat content or the large distributors that came by to pick it up with their tanker trucks wouldn't take it.

In the evenings, when I finally had time to cook, the breakfast dishes were still piled up in the sink. Owen and the kids would watch *Laugh-In* with Goldie Hawn and Arte Johnson while I worked in the kitchen, cleaning, scrubbing and doing the laundry. My own day began then; the cows got the rest of it. After living in a large, cozy house on Long Island, it felt like I was back in Germany during the war.

On top of it all, it was a bitterly cold winter. Some mornings, the snow that had fallen overnight was so deep that I couldn't walk from the house to the barn. I had to crawl on all fours until Owen or Dave made a path with the tractor.

The temperature dropped so low that the feed in the silo froze solid. Owen took a pickaxe to hack some pieces off, but he slipped and drove the point through his boot into his foot. We had to take him to the hospital to get patched up.

All of the equipment was old and kept breaking down. We were constantly having to fix it. It was always a struggle, but we managed somehow, and Owen was happy.

After school, the kids came home and helped. Dave was fourteen by then and pulled more than his weight. We had a manure wagon which he'd take out into the almost frozen fields to dump the load the cows made. If the wind came up, it would carry the stench right back into the barn. Sometimes, the cold manure would plug up the spreader and he'd have to clean it. More than once I heard him curse like a longshoreman. I could understand his frustration and never reprimanded him for swearing out loud.

Another time, he nearly scared me to death. We had found beautiful, old wall scones in the basement. I wanted to put them up in the bathroom, but the glass had been painted white, so little light shone through. Dave decided to clean them in the basement with paint thinner and a wire brush. I was in the kitchen when I heard him cry out, "Help! Help!" When I opened the door to downstairs, I saw an orange glow—his hands and arms were burning! Somehow, he had set the turpentine on fire. Perhaps the wire brush caused a spark. By the time Owen and I got there, the wooden work bench was ablaze, too. We managed to douse the flames and put ice on Dave's hands. Then, we rushed him to the hospital. Fortunately, he was all right. He healed fine and his ordeal left no scars.

Shirley had a more enjoyable experience. She would have liked to have a pony, but we didn't have the money for it. So, she did the next best thing. When the cows were in their stanchions, she climbed on them and pretended to ride them. She talked to them and gave them names like Salty, Bull Face, and Big Mama. When it was time to feed the cows, she and Dave climbed into the barn's hayloft and had fun tossing bales of hay down. The first time, we found out that the batch had gone bad and the heifers didn't want to eat it, so we had to buy molasses and mix it in with the hay to deceive them.

I hated the cows. They're dumb and stubborn creatures. They kick out if they don't want to cooperate as you move them from one place to another. I had to smack them with a rubber hose to get their heads into the stanchions for milking.

Christmas time was the worst because the kids were waiting to get their presents, but I had to keep working in the barn.

As spring came, we had more adventures.

There were a lot of feral cats in the surrounding fields and woods. One afternoon, Shirley saw one in the driveway. She went outside and called for it to come to her, but it didn't respond to her coaxing. When Shirley came to me, complaining that the "kitty" wouldn't play with her, I looked outside. Imagine my shock when saw a bobcat sitting there. Shirley had no idea how lucky she was to survive that encounter without serious bites and scratches.

One of the heifers had come to us pregnant and when she gave birth, I decided to wake up the kids so they could see it happening. It was the middle of the night, and Shirley got up, but Dave didn't want to come. We waited a long time until we saw hooves. Owen put on a rubber glove that came all the way to his armpit and thrust his hand inside the cow to help. He pulled the calf out by its legs and it plopped on the ground, a slimy, little heap. It was amazing, though how quickly it got up, standing on wobbly legs and taking its first, uncertain steps while the mother cow licked it clean. Since Shirley had watched it all, we told her she could name the calf, and because it wobbled when it first tried to run, she called him Skippy.

As I became increasingly exhausted and irritated, my fuse got shorter, too. I had never quarreled with my husband before, but at the barn, we argued and fought like crazy. I didn't think we would ever get the hang of what it took to make a go of it. We were big city folks with country dreams and no idea how to implement them.

Looking back on that time, Shirley liked to sayd, "It was like *Green Acres*, but not as funny."

One day, I had enough. In the morning after Shirley and Dave went to school, I said to Owen, "This isn't working out. Either the cows go, or I'm taking my kids and am leaving you."

It shocked him, but he listened when told him, "We'll have to work for at least five years to make money off this farm. By then, all of our savings will be gone. In the meantime, we can't afford to hire anyone to help. Our children are getting minimum attention already, and it will only get worse."

Owen looked at me, his lips tight. Then he closed his eyes to think. When he opened them, he said, "You're right.

He called an auctioneer, who came with his team and spruced up the cows' appearance. They washed and combed them and braided their tails. After cleaning the barn, they filled it with new straw. By the time the auction took place in April, Owen had gone back to Long Island to find a job. The cows looked beautiful, and one after the other was sold. I felt bad for the old ones because they were going to the slaughterhouse. When the wagon came to pick them up, Big Mama cried miserably as she climbed up the walkway into the back. Tears were running down the side of her face. Until then, I had no idea that cows could cry. It was like she knew she was going to die.

Mortified, I thought, "What am I doing?"

But I knew it was either them or me. So, I gritted my teeth and saw things through to the end until all the cows were gone. We sold all the machinery, too, even though some of it needed repair and didn't bring a very good price. Then, we put the house on the market with a local realtor while I still lived there.

In the meantime, Owen had gotten a job as head maintenance supervisor at Creedmoor, a large state psychiatric hospital in Queens. At some point, it served 7,000 patients. He lived in an apartment on the grounds, like many of the doctors, psychologists, and other healthcare professionals that worked there, and drove up the Taconic Parkway to Coxsackie on Saturday morning to spend the weekend. When he arrived, he took me shopping and I bought groceries for the week. He returned to Long Island late Sunday or early Monday morning.

We could have lived at Creedmoor, too, but Owen didn't want our children to be around so many people who suffered mental illnesses. So, he found a Cape Cod style house on Brennan Street in Huntington. It had four bedrooms, two bathrooms and was very nice, although the upstairs bedrooms were still unfinished. While Owen got the place ready, we remained at the farm.

To earn pocket money, Dave and his friend Danny baled hay for Mr. Dunmore who had a large dairy farm with more than a hundred heifers. On the weekends, they sometimes camped out overnight on the hill behind out farm, where the flint cave was located. They walked to the top, which was flat as a table, and pitched their tent. From there, they had a great view of the Hi-Way Drive-In Movie Theater across State Route 9W. Before they started their hike, they sneaked into the drive-in and turned up the car speakers. That way they could hear and see the movie playing from their perch when it got dark.

In May, my parents came from Germany to visit us. My father was looking forward to milking the cows as he had done when he was young, and he was disappointed that we had sold all of our livestock. He did enjoy climbing Flint Mine Hill with Owen and Dave to look at the cave—at that time his emphysema was still under control.

*My parents visiting us at the farm in front of
the brick house, summer of 1969.*

It was good to have them with us, good for my children, good for me. I liked hearing about what was happening to my relatives in Germany. Everyone seemed to be doing well. The only negative news was

126

that my brother had become more difficult. Horst was drinking a lot and was often abusive, cursing and breaking things. When my parents tried to intervene, he'd only get mad. His wife was afraid of him. After he sobered up, he would apologize for his behavior, but his promises to do better lasted only until the next time he went on a bender. It was heart wrenching to see my parents so unhappy about him.

They stayed for three weeks and I was sad to see them leave. With them gone, I had nothing to look forward to, only more of the same work and no respite in sight.

In early June, when it was time to for me and the children to return to Long Island, I hired movers. It was too much for me to do alone. The kitchen cabinets still sat in the middle of the empty room.

I rented out the farm house to a couple that had three children. I charged them $40 a month just for electricity because it was hooked up to the barn, which was also rented out—to a farmer who kept his cows there.

The people never paid me the rent. After a while, Owen said, "You better get the money from them."

But when I called, the husband hemmed and hawed. He was making a living salvaging things and selling them. In the end, I hired a lawyer, and after eight months, they were evicted, although I never saw a penny of the money they owed me.

The house sat empty for a while longer. When we finally managed to sell it, along with the rest of the property, our dairy farm adventure finally came to a close.

12
Moving On and Visiting

We lived in the house on Brennan Street as best we could. It was good to be back in Huntington and familiar surroundings. Over the winter, Owen built out the three rooms upstairs. That way, Shirley and Dave could have their own, separate bedrooms at opposite ends of the house. I used the middle room for my sewing and crocheting projects, making dresses and curtains.

Owen fixing up our house.

We settled in comfortably, and the following spring, Owen added a garage for our car.

Although, Owen had been disappointed that his farm experiment didn't pan out, he was never one to look back for long. As a supervisor at Creedmoor Hospital, he worked hard and was a popular boss. He started to teach courses in plumbing, carpentry, and electrics for the people who worked for him, allowing them to acquire new skills. He occupied himself with all kinds of projects and even helped Harold on some of his plumbing ventures.

Shirley and Dave were happy to back in school with their friends. I put in a garden in back and grew vegetables and flowers. We were living the American Dream.

Owen and me at Brennan Street.

In the spring of 1971, during Owen's two-week vacation, we visited Germany. It was the first time I went back since I had left, and a great deal had changed. The most obvious was the presence of the Wall the Soviets had built a decade earlier, dividing Berlin.

We took the S-Bahn and visited Checkpoint Charlie on Friedrichsstrasse with the big sign warning: YOU ARE LEAVING THE AMERICAN SECTOR. In contrast, the little guardhouse marking the border crossing between West and East Berlin looked small and unassuming. We walked right up to the concrete barrier that extended on either side and looked into East Berlin, where the ground was raked smooth and barren. The tall guard towers spaced every hundred feet or so were intimidating, as were the smirking, uniformed East German guards parading with machine guns slung over their shoulders.

To the right on Zimmerstrasse, in front of the Wall, stood a simple black cross surrounded by bouquets of flowers. It was the memorial for Peter Fechter, who was shot by East German border guards on August 17, 1962, as he tried to escape. He was only eighteen years old and bled to death for an hour, lying at the Wall, screaming an pleading as the guards refused to come to his aid.

There were double-decker buses for sightseeing tours of East Berlin, and Owen wanted to go. But I refused. Although I had an American passport, I was afraid I wouldn't be allowed to come back. I was too shaken by the cruelty of what had happened there.

On Weddingstrasse, all the rubble from the bombed-out houses had been cleared, but nothing had been built in their place. The area across the street from my parents' apartment house was just a big, empty lot. The government had fixed up the Kurfürstendam, as well as other high-end shopping areas and upscale residential districts, but it hadn't gotten to the back streets of the lower class neighborhoods yet. Some of the buildings' exteriors were pockmarked with grenade splinters and bullet holes from the war.

On the second floor of our building, there was a vacant room between the two apartments where Owen and I stayed. Shirley and David slept in my and Horst's old bedroom. It was crowded in my parent's living room, but cozy, and we talked late into the night.

For me the experience was familiar and strange at the same time. There were odors I hadn't encountered for seventeen years, like the smell of cooked cabbage in my parent's apartment house and the slightly sweet, musky aroma of the wax on the wooden stairs. Everything looked smaller, more confined, compared to the places I had lived in the United States.

The Sawadas still ran their deli downstairs. When I walked in, they recognized me right away and called out, "Trauty!" They came out from behind the counter and hugged me. They looked older but still energetic and outgoing, and they were happy to meet my husband and children. When I asked after their son, Kurt, they told me he was at the university, beaming with pride. Mrs. Sawada remembered my sweet tooth and asked if I wanted a macaroon. I smiled and said, "Yes, a pink one—strawberry!" It tasted just as good as I remembered.

We met my brother, Horst, and his wife, Ingrid, at the new garden cottage my parents had bought to the west of Siemensstadt in the Haselhorst area—my grandfather and his wife who had lived in the old cottage at Schiller Heights were no longer alive. Horst and Ingrid had three children by then, Guido, Axel, and Heike, who was still a baby. Their fourth came later. Axel was Shirley's age and they played together while the adults socialized. Horst and I hugged awkwardly and made conversation. We treated each other politely, like two distant acquaintances, not at all like brother and sister. Knowing about his frequent drinking bouts and irresponsible, abusive behavior, I was angry on behalf of my parents. They did not deserve that.

We had a more pleasant visit with my cousin Brigitte and her husband Dieter. They lived in a small apartment in the Moabit district, near my grandparents on my mother's side. Brigitte, was the youngest daughter of my Uncle Kurt, who had died at Stalingrad. After the war, when thing became too difficult for my aunt, taking care of six children on her own, my parents had wanted to adopt Brigitte, but the authorities did not grant them permission because we didn't have room enough in our apartment. Instead, she ended up living with her grandparents.

She and Dieter were childhood sweethearts—their birthdays are only one day apart: November 28 and 29. Although he was five years older than her, when they were young, they walked to and from school together, Dieter carrying her books. When she turned seventeen, he asked for Brigitte's hand in marriage. Her grandfather had to give his permission because she was not yet of age, but he had known Dieter for a long time and was glad to grant their wish.

Dieter worked at a large manufacturing plant of a company that produced baking goods. At the time of our visit, he was a manager. Some of his duties involved overseeing the storage of wheat and rye, making sure that the kernels didn't rot in their bins. They had two young daughters by then, Enith and Corolla, and Brigitte was sewing winter coats to make extra money.

They were generous people and visited my parents as often as they could, bringing them groceries, beer and soda, and whatever was needed. Dieter was a handsome, broad-shouldered man and strong as a bull. He would paint and fix broken things around my parents' apartment and their summer cottage. Their support helped my parents enormously, especially when my father became seriously ill; and later on, after he died.

Brigitte was very pretty, with blond hair and blue eyes and a nice figure. We have very different personalities—she is easy-going and calm; I am more intense. But during that first visit, we took to each other like old friends. In time, she and I became like sisters. It was the beginning of one of the most important friendships of my life.

If I felt any nostalgia for the past during our visit, it was soon erased when we went to see the leather goods store where I had worked. The original Gerloff & Sienholz shop was still there on Badstrasse, and when I entered, the familiar leather smell brought back emotions and almost overwhelmed me.

As it happened, Mr. and Mrs. Sienholz were both there. They had aged visibly, their faces wrinkled and their hair gray.

I walked up to the counter and said, "Do you remember me? It's Waltraut, from America."

A look of recognition crossed their faces, and Mr. Sienholz smiled. But when I introduced my husband and my children, Mrs. Sienholz looked at Owen imperiously and said, "Is it still the same one?"

I was too shocked by her poor manners to give a rude reply, but she reminded me of what I had gladly left behind—small-minded people putting on airs and acting superior, comparing themselves to others and lording their prejudices and values over them. I know it's not an exclusively German trait, but I certainly associate it with my time growing up there. Fortunately, that was our only negative experience.

One of the highlights was our trip to Vienna. We traveled on a charter bus, driving past meadows of red poppies and visiting castles along the way. All the other passengers were women in their 60s and 70s. Some had canes and walkers. When we started out, we sat in the rear of the bus and they paid no attention to us. At our first stop for the night, we all ate at the hotel restaurant. The women ignored us. Not a single one came over to our table to say hello. But then, Owen ordered a round of drinks for them and that broke the ice. They raised their glasses, toasted us, and called for us to join their circle.

There was a small band, and after Owen invited one of them to dance with him, they all wanted a turn. He was accommodating and danced with as many of the women as he could before promising the others, "Next time." From then on, we were all the best of friends.

In Vienna, we went to the famous Spanish Riding school and saw the magnificent, white Lipizzaner stallions perform in the baroque Hofburg Palace, which had been built in the early 1700s. Their grace and powerful manner left a lasting impression on my children and me.

We also visited Alpine castles high up in the mountains where Edelweiss covered the meadows on both sides of the road. Owen was especially interested in the craftsmanship of the builders and furniture designers. I always thought about the effort it must have taken to cart and carry all the stones and wood to such isolated places.

Traveling north on our own, we took a cruise on the Rhine and marveled at the castles perched on the steep hills on both sides of the river. One of my favorite tourist attractions was the Asbach Uralt factory in Rüdesheim. I was delighted to find out how my favorite brandy was made. In the visitor center, there was a table with snifters filled with the golden-brown brandy. Of course, I had to drink one, even though I hadn't had breakfast yet. When we toured the distillery, we saw hundred-year-old stills and copper fermentation vats. All in all, it was a wonderful trip, but I was glad to come back to the United States and what I felt was my real home now.

We lived on Brennan Street for another year. It was a pleasant stay for everyone.

To help make ends meet financially, I started to clean houses. My friend Fran Scalia who lived across the street had been doing that for some time herself, and I asked if she knew anybody else who could use my services. At her suggestion, I called several people and got a number of jobs. Fran dropped me off in the mornings wherever I had to go that day—I still didn't know how drive a car—and picked me up on her way home. She had five children and took a play pen along to her jobs so she could keep her two little ones with her while she worked.

Fran was a gem. She was a good ten years older than me and had grown up in Germany, too—in Munich. She and her husband, Joe, had met there after the war, gotten married, and come to the United States by boat. Although Bavarians (Southern Germans), and Berliners (Prussians) are not supposed to get along, we became best of friends.

One of my clients was Dr. O'Brien, a local GP who had his practice in his home in Greenlawn, the suburb immediately east of Huntington. He was a good twenty years older than me and generous and appreciative—a sweetheart of a man. He always paid me a bonus at Christmas. At some point, he sold us his 1969 Chevy Impala, which was in excellent condition.

I also cleaned for three older women who lived in Dix Hill, an upscale neighborhood southeast of Huntington. Their houses stood next to each other on the same street, and I'd clean one house one day, another the next, and so on. I also replaced fixtures and hung pictures for them. They liked what I did so much that they started to pick me up at my house when Fran couldn't drive me to work. One of them told me, "Why, Wally, if we had to, we'd drive to the next state to get you."

When Owen, the kids and I used to go a nearby farm stand on Saturdays and buy all our vegetables there, he invariably said, "We can grow these ourselves." He was always thinking about farming. He wanted a place with more land.

Dave, Shirley and me in the backyard garden on Brennan Street.

One day, I saw an ad in the *New York Times* for a house for sale in East Northport, a town just east of Huntington. I called up my father-in-law, and he drove me there. The house at 16 Teresa Lane was a split level that sat on half an acre. It was part of a community of similar, two-story homes. But while the others were well-kept, this one had tall grass growing in the yard and paint peeling off the shutters. Still, it seemed suitable. That evening, Owen and I went back to take a look and he liked it. By the time we told the realtor we wanted to buy it, he had already figured out what to do with it.

The house belonged to a man who had his hands full raising two daughters as a single dad and had let it fall into disrepair. Yet, his asking price of $44,000 was expensive. Owen knew that the place had to be painted before any bank would give us a mortgage, so he got the owner to take $2000 off the price. We cut the grass and painted the house ourselves. Later, after we moved in, all our neighbors on the street told us about the industrious people who had come to fix it up, not realizing that it had been us!

Our house on Teresa Lane.

We moved in as the former owner moved out. Owen's brother Billy helped cart all our furniture. We planned to camp out there until we put the rooms together. Coincidentally, Fran and her family had moved to the same neighborhood, just three blocks away on Elwood

Avenue. When she saw how dirty the house was inside, she said, "Wally, you can't let your kids sleep here." She took them to stay at her home until Owen, Billy, and I had finished bringing in all our furniture and making the place livable.

The house had a dining room, kitchen, playroom, laundry room, bathroom and a bedroom on the first floor, which became my husband's office. Five steps up was a monster-sized living room. Five more steps up were three more bedrooms and two bathrooms. The one for David and Shirley had two sinks. By then they were both teenagers and the arrangement worked out well.

We occupied our home early in 1972 and continued to make improvements. Owen installed wood paneling in the kitchen, which was all the rage then, recovered the cabinets with dark brown formica veneer, and built a tool shed in the backyard. I loved living there.

Dave, Shirley, Owen and me at Teresa Lane circa 1977.

In May of that year, Brigitte and Dieter and their two daughters came from Germany to visit us for the first time. We had a lot of fun taking trips to the eastern end of Long Island, and to the Finger Lakes in upstate New York, and to Niagara falls in upstate New York. We all crowded into one car, seven of us—Dave didn't go—and got along well, cementing our friendship.

Two years later, I went to Germany with Shirley. I was worried about my father because he had stopped sending me letters. He was all right, although his emphysema was getting worse.

West Berlin was changing, becoming a modern, international city again. I was happy to spend time with Brigitte and Dieter. By then, they had a garden cottage, too, in the Neuköln district. It was solidly constructed with bricks, and Dieter had finished the interior and installed all the newest appliances.

I enjoyed my visits to Germany, but I was always glad to come home to Teresa Lane. We were happy there. I continued to clean houses. Owen put in a big vegetable patch and a beautiful rose garden with an arbor. He definitely had a green thumb. He also planted all kinds of fruit trees. Soon, I supplied everyone in our neighborhood with our bounty of peaches, apples, nectarines, apricots and plums. We had vines growing on the fence surrounding the garden. In the summer, there was so much greenery in our backyard it felt like we were living in the country.

Me in the back of our house on Teresa Lane.

In 1974, my parent visited us for three months. We had a wonderful time with them, going to the beach and sightseeing in Manhattan.

We also heard about what was going on with my relatives. Not all the news was good. My brother Horst had continued to deteriorate. He had become an angry alcoholic and refused to get any help.

It was difficult to see my father struggle with his emphysema. Sometimes, it was impossible for him to walk it across the room without stopping to catch his breath. We kept an oxygen tank for him in case he needed it and a bottle of gin by his side. He insisted that his doctors had told him that liquor would open up the pores in his lungs and make it easier for him to breathe, and he took advantage of his "medicine" by having several shots during the evening. Yet, he always showed good spirits and never complained.

My parent' visiting in 1974. From left: Aunt Agnes;
my mother-in-law, Viola; my mother; me in back; Owen's uncle Carl,
who died at age 98; my father-in-law; and my father.

I wanted my parents to stay with us for good, but it wasn't feasible. In Germany, which had universal health insurance, my father could obtain all the medicine he needed for free. In the United States, he would have had to pay for it, and the costs would have been prohibitive. So, we saw them off at the airport in late August with hugs and kisses and their promises to return soon.

The following year, Owen built a big awning off the patio next to the kitchen so we had shade in the hot summer days.

For Christmas 1976, my parents visited us again, this time with my father's sister, Aunt Gertrude, who everyone called Trudchen. We went all out with gift giving that year. On Christmas Day morning, the living room overflowed with opened boxes and torn wrapping paper. My parents and Trudchen were amazed. They'd never seen so many presents.

Dave, me and Shirley on Christmas morning.

Owen was a good provider. He took care of everything, and more. The only thing he ever denied me was my dream of owning a flower shop. We always had flowers in our gardens. I would put them together in attractive arrangements to spruce up the interior of our house. For Christmas, I bought wreaths, decorated them, and gave them as presents to our neighbors. Many of them told me, "Wally, you should open a flower shop."

So I asked Owen, "Would you set me up with a flower shop?"

He said, "What do you need that for? We have plenty of flowers in the garden."

I kept asking him several times and always got the same reply. One time, I got so annoyed with him, I said, "Well, then let the florist come every week!"

We'd been having that argument at least once or twice a year. But after we moved to Teresa Lane, and we had our biggest garden ever, I grew a lot of roses and brought them into the house. I loved their smell and delicate blossoms. That satisfied my need to surround myself with natural beauty, and I stopped pestering my husband.

Time passed, and in the summer of 1979, my parents came for a visit with my brother's daughter Heike. On August 6, we celebrated my father's 70th birthday on the patio. All my in-laws came—Marie, Junie, Bill and their children, and Owen's parents. We had a big cake and a picnic table filled with food. The party went on long into the night.

That visit was the last time I saw my father.

By then, their building on Weddingstrasse was slated for demolition, and they had relocated to an apartment in Siemensstadt. It was closer to Brigitte and Dieter and their garden cottage, but they wanted to get out of Berlin. Aunt Trudchen lived in West Germany and found a suitable place for them right next door to her. It was in the country and when my parents visited, they fell in love with it—the fresh air, the birds, and the cows grazing in the nearby meadows.

So, they started to pack up their belongings. From what Brigitte told me, my father worked so hard he overexerted himself and developed water in his lungs. It got so bad he had to be taken to the hospital in an ambulance, and he died a few days later, on March 5, 1980, a week before my birthday.

When I got the call from Brigitte, I broke down in tears. Although I had expected it to happen for some time, when it did, it hurt so bad. I was inconsolable. I adored my father and I felt guilty that I had not been there to take care of him, despite all reassurances from my cousin that I had nothing to be sorry for. Next to Owen, he was the most important man in my life, and for him to be gone was devastating. It took me several months to regain my emotional balance and positive spirit.

In the meantime, the relationship between Owen and his brother grew increasingly testy. On one occasion, when he offered to help with putting in a heavy sink, Harold looked at him dismissively and said, "Oh no, you're much too old to do that."

My husband didn't say anything but felt like Harold had slapped him. That was the end of their relationship as far as Owen was concerned. He never got over it, and he brought it up in conversations with me a number of times—how much Harold's rejection had hurt him.

Of course, Harold was not a happy man himself. By then he and Moo had divorced. When their children left home, Moo went back to school and became a nurse. She met someone at the clinic where she worked, remarried, lived in another home in Huntington, and eventually moved to Florida.

Harold lived alone for some time and didn't like it. Then, he met Edith, who had three children from a previous marriage. After their wedding, they bought a house in Asharoken, an upscale neighborhood on the north shore of Northport Bay to the northeast of Huntington. We didn't see them very often.

One occasion we did was the 50th wedding anniversary of Owen's father and Viola. They were no longer in the best of health and decided to renew their vows. The ceremony was held in a meeting hall in Huntington, and the whole family attended.

Owen organized the whole thing and laid out the money for the various expenses. Everybody was supposed to contribute equally and pay him back for their share. All his brothers and sisters did ,except Marie, although she did take care of making all the calls to invite everyone.

It was a lovely event. Viola wore a wreath of roses. Owens father had bought new rings and they placed them on each other's fingers. During the party afterward, Harold knelt before his mother and sang "Danny Boy" to her. It was her favorite song even though she didn't have an Irish bone in her body. But he put his heart into it, and it was very moving. Everyone became teary eyed.

Owen, his father, mother, and me after the ceremony.

Viola died a year later. My father-in-law followed in short order, dying on the operating table when his doctors tried to install a new pacemaker. Although he put on a good outward appearance, he didn't get over losing his wife and felt he had nothing to live for anymore. The funerals for both were somber affairs, as if a big chapter of the Stanton family had come to a close. Owen mourned his parents for many months.

But not all events during those years were so heart-rending. In July of 1981, Shirley got married to Tony. She had been working in a nursing home and a co-worker wanted to introduce her to him, but for the longest time Shirley said No. Finally, she relented and they went on a blind date, and liked each other. That happened in August of 1980. Tony worked for AAMCO, and subsequently for Midas

Muffler. Later, he became a member of a construction trade union in New York, working for 33 years until his retirement. He always was a good provider for his family and did his job in all types of weather conditions, rarely missing a day of work

Meanwhile, the following year on her birthday, Shirley told me they were engaged. A month later, they got married.

The wedding took place in the Huntington Town House, an elaborate building complex with three large ballrooms, each with its own catering kitchen and bandstand, and separate dressing rooms for the brides. It was the favorite venue for wedding receptions, proms, and other events in the area. A chapel upstairs on the third floor accommodated couples that wanted a non-church ceremony, which worked out well because Tony was raised Catholic and Shirley was not.

My mother came from Germany. She had bought herself a princess dress for the occasion, white with little black flowers. She told all her friends proudly, "I'm going to America to my granddaughter's wedding!"

Everything went according to plan until the minister who was to officiate the ceremony had a heart attack on the way to the Center. Huddling with the owners of the place, the bride and groom decided open the cocktail bar prior to the ceremony until they could find a replacement. Meanwhile, Tony's cousin got on the phone and called the churches around town. It took nearly two hours before she found an Episcopalian priest who agreed to come. By then, the Town House staff had located a willing chaplain as well. Now, there were two ministers. Fortunately, the were good-natured about it and figured out how to collaborate on the ceremony.

By the time Owen walked Shirley down the aisle, the 125 wedding guests were suitably happy. Shirley had had a drink, too, and was understandably nervous. So when the priest said, "Does anyone object to these two getting married," she jumped the gun and said, "I do." Everyone laughed and from that point on everything went without a hitch. Everyone enjoyed the four-hour reception that followed, and Shirley and Tony left for their honeymoon weekend at Villa Roma in the New York Catskills.

From left: Owen, me, Tony, Shirley, my mother, and Owen's father.

The minister who had a heart attack recovered, too. The following day, an article about the wedding came out in *Newsday*, the daily paper for Long Island and New York City, with the headline, "Chaplain Leaves Couple Waiting at the Altar."

13

Heart-Break

The following year, Owen started to cough. When his condition started to get worse, I asked him to see a doctor. He agreed but always found a reason not to go.

One night in September, he went upstairs to take a shower and came back wearing his burgundy bathrobe and slippers—we had gotten them for him on his birthday. He lay down in front of the television and kept coughing.

Standing behind his recliner, I said, "You didn't keep your appointment with the doctor."

"I don't need a doctor," he replied. "You know what I have."

"What do you have?" I asked.

"I got the big C," he spat out. He sounded really angry.

"What do you mean?"

"Cancer!"

He was right: It was lung cancer. He had smoked cigarettes when I met him in Germany and in his construction business, although he was never a chain smoker. Doing a lot of the work himself, he breathed in asbestos and fiberglass from putting insulation into walls and ceilings, and the fumes from pouring liquid lead into plumbing pipe joints. Although he quit cigarettes for a while and pursued a better life style, doing isometric exercises and eating healthy food like wheat germ and the vegetables we grew, he started smoking again in the late 1970s working at Creedmoor.

The doctors prescribed chemotherapy and, for the time being, Owen kept going to work while I continued to clean houses. But the first round of chemo didn't help and he had to have another. After the New Year, he started to decline and couldn't do his job anymore.

It got so bad Owen couldn't lie down and had to sit up even when he slept. I got the chaise lounge from the patio for him during the day and propped him up with pillows in his bed at night. At some point, he couldn't walk up the stairs anymore. We converted the downstairs office into his bedroom. Finally, I got a hospital bed and a wheelchair with a portable oxygen canister. He had a cane by his side and would knock on the bed with it for me to come. He didn't want to be alone. He was afraid. After a while, I put a cot by his door and spent the night there.

In the afternoons, when the weather was sunny, I would take Owen in the wheelchair around the neighborhood. Shirley often came to spend time with him after work. She and Tony lived in an apartment only two blocks away.

Owen rallied for Dave's wedding in April of 1983.

Dave had dated a young woman, Maria, for a year and a half. Her father was a television editor for NBC in New York, and she worked there, too, as a graphic artist on various shows, commuting to and from the city every day.

Maria's parents put a lot of money and effort into the wedding and paid for everything. It took place at the Huntington Town House in Huntington. Maria's parents had the affair catered and hired a band to play. Marie knew calligraphy and did all of the invitations herself. Everyone complimented her about them. Her wedding dress was gorgeous, and everyone agreed that the ceremony was lovely. Afterward, she and Dave moved into an apartment a couple of miles from where we lived.

Dave and Owen at the wedding.

In many ways, that event was Owen's last hurrah. His health continued to deteriorate to the point where he couldn't eat solid food anymore. He could only sip nourishing drinks, and he had difficulty breathing.

Our neighbors in the houses on either side of ours were wonderfully supportive. Because I didn't have the time to cook anymore, they did it for me and brought me dishes.

One night, when Owen couldn't breathe, I gave him oxygen, but it didn't help. After I called the ambulance, I telephoned Shirley and Dave, and we all went to the hospital. We sat in the waiting room. I could hear him screaming and got very upset. When the doctor came out of the examining room, he explained to us that they had to put a breathing tube down his throat. Owen was plugged up with so much mucus that it hurt terribly.

I stayed with him in his room all day long and went home at night. He couldn't talk anymore because of the tube in his throat, but he communicated with the nurses and us using a writing pad. He had always liked music and asked for a radio so he could listen to opera. He'd never expressed an interest in that kind of music before, but the nurses did as he wished and brought a tape recorder. The music relaxed him. Dave, Shirley, and I sat there and listened with him, held his hand, and talked to him. Sometimes Maria visited, too.

The doctors knew that Owen was dying. I knew it, too.

On June 11, a Saturday, I was at the house waiting for my son to come home from the gas station where he worked as an auto technician and drive me to the hospital. The phone rang. I picked it up and the nurse at the other end told me that Owen had died. I burst into tears and nearly collapsed on the floor.

When I recovered, I called Dave. He came right over and we went to the hospital. The staff had removed the breathing tube, but Owen no longer looked like the man I'd known. The life force was gone and only his physical body was left.

I called my mother in Germany. She got on a plane as soon as she could with one of my brother's sons, my nephew Axel. They arrived two days later. Her being there gave me the support I needed to get through it all.

As we made the funeral home arrangements, Owen's supervisor at Creedmoor asked me to extend the viewing time to three days. All of the men Owen had worked with wanted to come because he had looked out for them. They held him in such high regard and all came the first day. The second day, friends and neighbors attended. The third day was for us, the immediate family.

We buried Owen on Tuesday, June 14, at the Northport Rural Cemetery. We had the service with my children and their spouses, my mother and nephew Axel, Harold and Edith, and Owen's sisters Junie and Marie. His brother Billy who lived in Florida by then didn't come to the funeral. Afterward, we gathered for a family get-together at Harold's house in Asharoken, and he was kind enough to offer me his condolences and assure me that he would give me any help I needed.

That Thursday was Shirley's birthday. She didn't want to celebrate it, but I insisted. My mother and Axel had come all the way from Germany, and I thought it was important for all of us to act like life would go on. It was a small, subdued party, but I'm glad we had it.

Dave came over to my house that Friday and kept me company. Maria didn't arrive home from Manhattan until after 7 p.m. He and I being both New York Yankee fans, we watched a baseball game together on television.

The next evening, he telephoned as I was getting ready for bed. I was upstairs when he called.

He said, "Mom, are you sitting down?"

I said, "What's the matter?"

"Are you sitting down?"

So, I sat on the bed and told him, "Yes."

With a choking voice, he said, "Maria left me. She took her personal belongings, our checkbook, along with some furnishings and some wedding gifts her family gave her and went home to her parents."

I told him to come over to my house. He was crying when he arrived. We sat in the living room and he told me that he had worked a half-day on Saturday, as usual, and when he got home that afternoon, there was a yellow pad on the kitchen table with a note from Maria, saying she didn't want to be married anymore and that he shouldn't try to contact her. She offered no explanation why she left and took half of their belongings with her. Obviously, it had not been a spur-of-the-moment decision because her family must have come to help her move out.

Dave had jumped in his car and driven to her parent's house. Maria's father met him at the front door but refused to let him see her.

Needless to say, my son was devastated. He had just lost his father two weeks earlier, and now his wife had abandoned him, too. After he moved back into my house, on more than one occasion, he went into the backyard and shouted at the top of his voice, "Why, why!"

It took Dave took a long time to accept that any relationship with Maria was over. A year later, with the help of a good attorney, their marriage was dissolved due to "irreconcilable differences," and an annulment was granted. We never found out what happened with Maria. It has remained a mystery to everyone in my family.

Fortunately, Dave recovered and got on with his life.

I tried to do so, as well, but it was hard. My mother who had stayed on after Owen's funeral said, "Trauty, you need to get away. You're coming to Germany with me."

So, I went to Berlin for five weeks. I saw Brigitte and Dieter, said hello to the Sawadas, and walked around the cities, looking at the places where I grew up, went to school, and worked. I also revisited the spots where Owen and I had met and spent time together. I was in a melancholy mood most of the time, cheering up only in the presence of other people.

At some point, my mother said, "Why don't you move back here to Berlin?"

I thought about it for a moment and said, "I can't. I have my children to consider. The United States is my home now."

I hated to disappoint my mother. I could tell she wasn't happy with my answer, but I meant what I said. I had become an American for good.

For me, Owen's death was a terrible tragedy. He was only fifty-four years old when he was taken from me—much, much too young; much

much too soon. We were married for twenty-nine years. He was the love of my life. I will be buried next to him.

Owen and me at Dave's wedding.

14

Life Goes On

By the time I returned to the United States, Dave had settled back into his sister's room at my house. The arrangement was convenient for him since he worked at an auto service center just around the corner. It was good for me, too, because there were times when being alone in a large home was difficult to bear. Dave also pitched in, mowing the grass, taking out the garbage, and taking care of things around the house.

I started to clean houses again. That paid for groceries but wasn't nearly enough to take care of incidentals and a mortgage of $300 a month. Although I was getting money from investments that Owen had made and Dave helped out, too, I knew I couldn't keep the house under those circumstances.

Fortunately, Owen's brother Harold had an idea. We put our heads together and decided to convert my son's old room and the space above the garage into a small apartment with a bedroom, living room, bathroom, and dinette kitchen. A staircase going up on the side of the garage to a new door created a separate entrance. Harold did all the construction, but he wasn't as generous as he'd promised to be. I ended up paying for everything.

When the apartment was finished, I rented it out to a young man who worked in a nearby flower shop. I'd met him a while back and knew he was well-groomed, dependable, and quiet. He often worked late and spent some nights at his parents' place, which was only a few blocks away. The extra income helped a lot.

I was still grieving and often felt inconsolable. Evenings were the hardest. During the day, I kept busy, but at night, even with the television on and Dave for company, the house felt empty and desolate. I missed Owen terribly and didn't know what to do with myself.

I was glad that Dave was moving on, though. One of his friends, Artie, told him that his wife had a girlfriend named Rosemary who was an airline flight attendant. She and Dave would be a good match. Rosie, as everyone called her, lived in Manhattan, but she would come to Artie's house on Long Island for dinner, and Dave could meet her there.

That night, my son came home complaining that he wasn't interested in going on a blind date. But after I talked to him for a while, he agreed, grudgingly. The dinner at Artie's house was a success. Everyone had a good time playing Trivial Pursuit until two in the morning! Dave and Rosie started to date and got along very well. After a while, he introduced us. I liked her right away. She was very businesslike, very professional, which matched his perfectionism. But she was also personable and fun to be around. I had turned Owen's downstairs bedroom into guest room for visitors from Germany, and Rosie often stayed there between her flight assignments.

By then, Shirley and Tony announced that they were pregnant. She was due in spring of the following year. In May, I organized a baby shower for her. Wouldn't you know it, she went into labor two days early and delivered a beautiful daughter, Diana.

By the time the baby shower took place, all her friends had frantically exchanged the pale yellow and lime-green outfits—this was before you could determine the gender of the baby ahead of time—and the room was covered in pink!

That fall, I took some baby steps myself and went out in public again, too. One day, when I was talking with one of my neighbors over the fence in the backyard, she said, "We're going out tonight, Wally. Why don't you come with us?"

I asked, "Where are you going?"

"Dancing. Come on. You need a night out."

Well, I loved to dance, so I decided to give it a try.

I put on one of my best dresses, and my neighbor, along with two other women, drove to a VFW meeting hall in Huntington. It was late fall and getting cold outside. By the time we got there, things were in full swing. We paid the entrance fee at the door and went inside. It was a big place with long tables and chairs surrounding an open area on three sides. At the other end, on a raised platform, a band played loud, upbeat music—disco, boogie-woogie, and popular hits.

There was a make-shift bar in the corner where you could buy Coca Cola, Seven-Up, and alcoholic drinks. People were sitting at the tables, some alone, some in groups, talking and watching couples on the dance floor. I was surprised how many single people were there. All the men wore suits and the women had put on their most elegant clothes. I realized I needed to upgrade my wardrobe. My dresses, though of good quality, were a bit dated by comparison.

When newcomers got up to dance to break the ice, the organizers made them stand in two lines—the men on one side, the women on the other—and they'd partner with whoever was across from them.

At some point, I noticed a man at a nearby table glancing at me. I looked back and our eyes met. He was handsome, dark-haired, and had an amiable smile. I got up and went to the ladies' room to make sure I looked all right. I was ready and wanted to dance with him.

So, when it was our turn, I counted where he was in line and made sure I got myself in the position opposite him. The band played the

155

Hustle, my favorite—I liked the rumba and foxtrot, too—and I took it as a good sign. He was a good dancer, and we twirled and shuffled like we had been together for years.

Afterward, he introduced himself. His name was Charles Calandra. We chatted for a while, and he asked me for my phone number. I didn't give it to him, but I took his. Then, we danced some more and agreed to meet up again the following week. That evening went well, too, and we started to date regularly.

There were different groups that held dances, including "Parents without Partners" and "Widows and Widowers," so there were plenty of opportunities to go out together. The events took place in church basements and big meeting rooms around town. There was always a bar and, on occasion, a table with snacks. Sometimes big bands played, sometimes only trios, but the music was always lively with a few slow numbers thrown in.

You couldn't go in as a couple, though. After Charly picked me up and we arrived at the dance hall, I would go inside first. He would wait a while before following me. We'd sit at separate tables near each other and after a while, he would ask me to dance. Then, we could sit together for the rest of the evening. A lot of couples did that.

It was a lot of fun. I had so much pent-up energy I felt we could go on all night. Charly was quite the gentleman. When there was ice or snow outside, he'd carry me from the car to the entrance foyer of the dance hall because I wore open shoes. We got to know a lot of the regulars and sat together and socialized.

Charlie was fifty-six years old, the same age as Owen. He'd been a police officer in Brooklyn for twenty-one years. After Charly retired from the force, he became a security guard at an IRS office building. Working late at night, he was making good money—we went out mostly on the weekends. He had a house in East Islip on the southern shore of Long Island across the bay from Fire Island, a half-hour drive from where I lived.

Charly had four grown children and had lost his wife, Theresa, to breast cancer the same month Owen died. After we got closer, I introduced him to Dave and Shirley and met his two daughters and two sons, Doreen, Theresa, Charles, and Robert. They did their best to be polite but didn't say much, and when they did, Charly usually interrupted them. Even though they were all adults, he was very controlling—the boss of the family.

Around that time, Dave decided that I really should get my driver's license. How else was I going to take care of myself and go shopping on my own when he moved out of my house? I agreed. He took me to an empty parking lot one night, and I drove around. I felt comfortable and relaxed with him and was getting the hang of it. By then automatic transmissions made it unnecessary to know how to shift gears manually. When Charly got wind of what was happening, he offered to give me lessons, too. That didn't go nearly as well because I put too much pressure on myself. After two unproductive outings, I finally went to a driving school and took professional lessons. That did the trick and gave me the confidence to finally pass the driving test and get my license.

At some point, Charly asked me if I wanted to go to Florida with him for a week or two. It turned out, we both owned property in Port Saint Lucie. Owen had purchased six lots and planned to build a vacation home there for us. (I later gave Shirley and Dave one of the properties each and sold the rest.)

Charly and I flew to Fort Lauderdale, rented a car, and shared a motel room by the beach. The weather was great, and we had a good time, lounging by the pool, tanning in the sun, swimming in the Atlantic Ocean, and going to bars and restaurants at night. I liked Charly's company, and I liked him. We had fun together.

Being away from home allowed me to relax and take stock of my situation. My birthday was coming up in March—I would be fifty-one—and didn't want to be alone anymore.

One morning after breakfast, Charly and I were in our motel room. He was looking through the real estate section of the local paper and said, "There are some nice places here. Maybe we should buy a house."

Surprised, I asked, "Do you want to move down here?"

He said, "Yes, I'd planned to retire here with Theresa."

"Me and Owen, too," I said. "He would have become a maintenance man here." Then I looked at Charly and said, "Are you going to marry me or not?"

He didn't miss a beat. "Yeah, I want to marry you."

"Well, then tell me. I don't want to wait forever."

So he asked me to marry him, and I said yes.

When we got back to Long Island, we made arrangements, getting our blood tests and applying for a wedding license. Two months later on June 3, 1985, we got married at city hall by ourselves, and I became Mrs. Calandra.

Afterward, we invited our children for dinner and sprung the news on them. None of them were surprised. Shirley said she knew something was up. But they all offered their congratulations and seemed genuinely pleased for us. Then, we told them that we would be moving to Florida. Before we left there, we had put money down on a condo in Margate, a small community east of Pompano Beach between Fort Lauderdale and Boca Raton. That news wasn't met with quite the same enthusiasm, but all of our children took it in stride. They knew we would do what we wanted anyway.

By then, Dave and Rosie's relationship had developed to the point that they had rented an apartment together in Glen Oaks in Queens. Not having to worry about him anymore, I put my house up for sale.

It was on the market for only two-and-a-half weeks when a couple from Brooklyn bought it, furnishings and all. The separate apartment was a big plus. They wanted to have the husband's mother live with them and brought her along when they came to see the place. She loved it, and that settled it.

Charly and I piled what we wanted to take with us into his Ford Taurus—clothes, pictures, odds and ends, mementos. I divided my extensive collection of German Beer Steins, from miniatures to two-foot tall mugs, and gave them to Shirley and Dave. Then, we said our good-byes to friends, neighbors, and our children, and headed south over the Verrazano Bridge for the Sunshine State.

Two days later, we arrived in Margate. We stayed in a motel until we closed on our condo. It was a two-bedroom unit, with a kitchen, living room, dining room, and a screened-in, outdoor patio. Freshly painted and empty, it looked bright, sunny, and inviting.

Our apartment was located on the second floor of a two-story building. Stairs led to an exterior landing and the entrance doors to the condos. You could see the parking lot from the kitchen. Our living room and patio overlooked fairways of the Carolina Club Golf Course. There were nine, two-story buildings altogether in a 92-unit complex that was part of Holiday Springs Village. We had access to a community swimming pool, an exercise room, and a clubhouse which had lots of activities and live entertainment every Saturday night.

Going shopping for furniture with Charly was an adventure and revealed how different our personalities were. He was always in a hurry. If we saw something and I said, "That's kind of nice," he jumped on it right away and said, "We'll buy it!"

But making snap decisions created difficulties down the road. When we bought a dining room set for four people, we soon discovered that it wasn't big enough for entertaining. So we had to replace it with a bigger one. Because I wanted something soft to sit on, we purchased a love seat and a beige couch. But while the sofa looked great, it turned out to be so mushy that people sank into it and had a hard time getting back up. I added big, puffy pillows to make it easier, but nothing ever really worked. Then, there were the two end tables we liked but hadn't measured, so only one fit in the living room.

Charly shopped the same way when we went to the supermarket to buy groceries. It was always: look, pick them out, and hurry up! Although I wasn't comfortable with that kind of approach, I learned to live with it.

He could be controlling, too. I was perfectly capable of driving a car now, but I didn't like the Ford Taurus we had. It got better when we bought a Buick Regal and, later on, a Mercury Cougar. Still, Charly preferred to do most of the driving. When I wanted to do errands or go to the hairdresser, he often said, "I'll take you." Then, he'd ask me how long I would be there and insisted, "You'll call me when you're done, and I'll come back for you."

The rare times he let me behind the wheel, he sat in the passenger seat and constantly gave me directions. "Don't you think you should turn your blinker on," he'd say as I turned at the entrance to our parking spot, even though no one was in back of me. Or he'd admonish, "Slow down," or "Move over into the next lane." I was nervous enough already, and he made it worse.

When we went up north to visit our children, Charly always insisted on doing all the driving. The first time we returned was for Dave's and Rosie's wedding in October of that year. When we arrived, Long Island was under a hurricane warning. Many people had left their homes, seeking shelter in hotels and motels, so we had a difficult time finding accommodations. We had to go far afield and finally got a room in a "no-tell" motel in Riverhead, thirty miles east of

Huntington. Most of the guest there rented rooms by the hour, and we were kept up all night by the noises made by an energetic couple next door.

But the wedding at a Presbyterian Church was lovely. The reception took place at the Crest Hollow Country Club in Woodbury, a different place than where Dave and Maria had gotten married. That wiped away all the negativity of the earlier relationship for good.

By then, I had met Rosie's mother, who had lost her husband when she was in her early forties. She'd raised three lovely daughters as a single mom without complaint, and I admired her for it. Rosie had many uncles and cousins who attended, making for a happy, boisterous crowd. We all had a good time.

The next day, we returned to Florida.

The following year, we had to drive back up north because Shirley was pregnant with her second child. But while we were waiting for her to go into labor, Charly got impatient. He insisted on going home, claiming that Shirley had plenty of support without me. I was furious and didn't say a word to him for the two days it took us to drive back to Margate.

Shirley had Anthony a week later, and I was happy to see him for the first time when we visited that Christmas. By then, Charly and I were on the best of terms again.

Over the next few years, we had a good time living at Margate. There was always something going on at the clubhouse and swimming pool, and we made lots of friends. At dinners, residents placed little flags on their table, indicating their ethnic backgrounds, and we discovered that there were many Italian-American couples from New York and Philadelphia. Charly was charming and gregarious and made friends with them easily.

We became especially close to three couples—Vera and Sam, Rose and Rocky, and Anne and Frank. They were terrific people. We played card games at each other's apartments, went to Diana Ross and Frank Sinatra concerts in Miami, and traveled on cruises together. They were ten or more years older than us, and Charly acted as chauffeur, bringing them to our place or picking them up for a night out.

Sam owned a landscaping business in Pittsburgh which he'd taken over from his father. Vera took care of all the paperwork. She and I often went shopping together. She had a great eye for good, stylish clothes, and I learned a lot from her.

Rose and Rocky were a good-looking couple. Rocky could be very funny and often had us all in stitches. He was as handsome as a movie star. Whenever we went on a cruise, women would gather around him, waiting to dance with him. Rose kept herself outfitted with fancy clothes and jewelry. She was attractive looking, too, and acted like a real beauty.

Anne and Frank were in a different class from everyone else. They were quite wealthy, but never put on airs. The liked us, and we liked them.

During the day we'd go to the malls and spent time on the beach. Charly liked to play golf, too. He found regular partners, Edith and Tom. He was Italian, she was Jewish, and both were on their second marriage. We became good friends with them, too.

One time, we all went to Las Vegas and from there to the Snake River for whitewater rafting through Hell's Canyon. It was one of the most barren places on Earth I've seen. I let my friends talk me into going, reminding myself of what Owen had said to me the first time we met—"Don't Be Afraid."

At the staging area for the rafts, the river was calm and smooth. After I put on my life jacket, I asked the guide, "Is the water very cold, if I fall in?"

He grinned and said, "If you fall in, you're dead."

That wasn't very reassuring, but I decided to get into the inflated, red-orange raft anyway. At first, I held to the sides with clenched fist, the way I always clutched the edge of swimming pools. But as we floated down the river, I started to relax and enjoy myself, even when we hit whitewater. By the end, I'd let go of a lifelong anxiety of drowning in water that had started when my brother's friends had dumped me in the *Plötzsee* forty years earlier. I was proud that I conquered that fear.

15

A New Germany

On November 9, 1989, the Berlin Wall came down and with it, the Soviet Empire. It seemed to happen all of a sudden, without warning. None of my relatives in West Berlin had an inkling it was coming. I watched the images on television in amazement—people sitting and standing on top of the concrete barrier, milling about, cheering, waving the German flag, while others knocked big holes in it with sledgehammers or toppled whole sections of the Wall.

I felt a warm light glow inside me all day long. When I called my mother in Germany, she and her friends were just as elated. They had not thought it possible that they would see the Wall come down in their lifetime.

I couldn't wait to visit the new Germany and look up relatives in the eastern half of the city, which I had not seen since after the war. So I was excited when Charly and I decided to traveled to Berlin in the summer in 1990.

When we got to the apartment of Dieter and Brigitte, they sent us to a hotel in Charlottenburg, where we stayed in a beautiful room. For the remainder of our visit, they drove us around in their BMW.

There was a flea market where you could buy Russian uniforms and helmets, pieces of the Wall that had been torn down, and pictures with stones from the Wall pasted on. I brought one of those home with me.

The best part for me was going to see my cousins in what had been East Berlin. You could tell right away how run-down that part of the city was. The streets had potholes, and the facades of buildings looked like they were from the late 1940s, after the war. In some places, we still could see grenade splinters on the sides of buildings, remnants from the fighting that had taken place in the last days of the Nazi defeat. In contrast to West Berlin, where everything had been repaired and rebuilt from scratch, it felt like traveling back in time, and lots of memories inundated me from the time when we returned from Luckenwalde to visit my mother's sister in Babelsberg.

At first, it felt awkward and strange to be with people I hadn't seen in forty-five years. They had lived under the Russian occupation for decades, and although they were the same age as Charly and me, they looked a lot older. And some of the stories they told were hard to believe. Berndt, Aunt Gertrude's son, for example, had worked in a factory, but there were no raw materials, so he and the others sat around on wooden boxes and played cards, and got paid for their time.

Brigitte and Dieter drove us to the Autobahn on the outskirts of Berlin to show us the automobile graveyard, hundreds of abandoned cars parked on both sides of roadbed on the grassy slopes. They were Trabants—Trabbies as the Germans called them—the cars the East German government had manufactured for its citizens. When people signed up for one, they had to wait ten years for delivery! With little else to buy, they saved their money. Now that they were free and had a nice little nest egg, they wanted to buy Mercedes, VWs, Audis, and BMWs. So, they just left their Trabbies by the side of the road.

At one point, we came upon someone whose car had broken down. He had the hood of his Trabbie up and was trying to start the motor We stopped, and Dieter and Charly got out to help. They did what they could, but to no avail. We finally left when the man threw up his hands in frustration and said he would call someone to pick him up and have his car towed.

When they got back in the car, Charly said to me, "The motor inside that car is no bigger than your sewing machine."

We all had a good laugh about that.

One evening, we joined Dieter for his weekly bowling outing. Many Germans like to go *kegeln*. They use only nine pins and smaller balls with no finger holes, but they have just as much fun as their American counterparts. Guzzling plenty of beer helps, too. Charly was feeling gregarious and bought everyone a round. I enjoyed myself. We must have made quite an impression because, according to Dieter, after that night, his friends often asked how I was doing in America.

It was good to spend time with my mother again, although the stories she told about my brother were upsetting. Horst had deteriorated further, getting drunk with greater frequency, terrorizing his family and becoming increasingly self-destructive.

He came over to my mother's apartment and demanded money. When she didn't give him any, he swore at her. Once, he called the police on her. When they arrived, he opened his shirt and showed them a bleeding gash across his chest and claimed that my mother had cut him. Fortunately, they didn't believe him. They realized that his injury was self-inflicted.

It got so bad that she no longer let him into her apartment. He would stand outside, calling up from the street, pleading with her, and banging on the entrance door of the building.

I was horrified. My mother did not deserve such treatment. I was relieved that Horst never hurt her, although she told me that he had hit his wife on several occasions. It made me so angry that I refused to see him. Only in retrospect did I feel bad for him, realizing that as an alcoholic, he was out of control and must have hated himself so much that he lashed out at everyone.

Except for that revelation, our trip was wonderful, and I flew home satisfied. After the Wall came down, people were optimistic about the future, hopeful that Germany could restore freedom and opportunities to all of its citizens.

That fall, on October 3, 1990, East and West Germany reunited officially as the Federal Republic of Germany. It was a big deal, and I felt proud again of the country where I'd grown up. I only wished my father was still alive to see it.

But, while Charly and I had an enjoyable visit, my relationship with him was no longer functioning well. Our honeymoon had been over for a long time, and we spent many days bickering or giving each other the cold shoulder. He became increasingly controlling and jealous. I had to watch what I said to him at all times. One time, at a potluck at the clubhouse, when I had brought a dish of asparagus, a young man complimented me on it and asked how I had prepared it. I told him what I had done, and he thanked me.

After he left, Charly came up to me, scowling suspiciously. "Who was that? What did he want?"

When I explained to him that the man had only asked for a recipe, he looked at me like he didn't believe me. He was certain that there was more going on, that the man must have had ulterior motives.

Everything for him seemed to revolve around money, and he became increasingly stingy. Before we got married, we decided to keep our finances separate, although we pooled our resources for the Margate condo and whenever we bought a new car. Because of Owen's investments and the sale of my house in Huntington, I brought more money into the marriage, and Charly resented it. He made me promise never to tell his children about the actual state of our finances.

We had a shared bank account for living expenses. Each month, we put in an equal amount to take care of incidentals, the mortgage, and condo maintenance fees. When I brought groceries home, Charly always looked through them. If I had bought a magazine or skin cream or lipstick, he'd ask, "How much was that?" and expect me to pay for them on my own—every little item I purchased for myself, he put on my bill.

Meanwhile, I was taking care of everything in the household. I dusted and cleaned, did the laundry, shampooed the carpet, and washed the dishes. After dinner, Charly would get up from the table and go into the bedroom, leaving the plates and silverware for me to clear. He treated me like I was his housekeeper.

During the summer months, things got worse because many of our friends went up north to escape the Florida heat and humidity and to visit their children. That left us isolated, with no one else to turn to. I began to feel that I had made a terrible mistake. Ours wasn't a real marriage anymore.

One Saturday in August of 1992, Charly went to a deli and picked up roast beef, bread, and rolls for lunch. When he came back, we ate on the patio. Afterward, he got up as usual and said, "I'm going to lie down for a while." He sprawled on the couch in the living room in front of the TV. I stayed outside, looking out over the golf course. Hurricane Andrew had blown through two weeks earlier, devastating entire neighborhoods of Miami. Fortunately, we had escaped unscathed, but some of the debris, uprooted trees and torn branches, hadn't been cleared from the fairways yet.

When I went into the kitchen to start cooking dinner, Charly got up and headed for the bedroom, saying, "You know what? You can watch your program and I'll watch mine." That suited me just fine.

At some point, when I heard him cough, I called out to him, "Are you all right?"

He yelled back, "Yeah, I'm fine."

But when he continued to cough and make odd sounds, I looked in on him and became alarmed. His face was ash colored as if drained of blood, and he was sweating even though the air conditioning was going full blast. Over his protests, I called 9-1-1, and the paramedics came in a hurry. They checked him out and said, "We have to take him to the hospital. It's probably a heart attack."

I followed them downstairs and watched as they put Charly in the ambulance. When they tried to hook up an IV, it took them some time to find a vein in his arm, irritating him further.

I was frightened. All my friends were up north. I had no one to turn to for help. The men from the fire department who'd come, too, gave me a ride to the hospital. Not long after I got there, two doctors came out of the examining room.

One of them said, "Mrs. Calandra, your husband has had a heart attack. A severe one." The other one asked, "Has he ever had one before?"

I said, "I don't think so."

They looked at me with a puzzled expression. I found out later that they were right to do so—Charly had had heart attack when he was still married to his first wife. He was taking medication his daughter-in-law got for him. He had told his male golf buddies with whom he hung out at the swimming pool, but he had kept it a secret from me.

Meanwhile, the doctors explained that his heart was in such bad shape that he needed a new one. They asked if we had an elevator where we lived because it would be impossible for him to climb stairs after a heart transplant. Our condo complex didn't, and I started to panic, thinking about having to sell our place and buying an apartment somewhere on the ground floor.

But it never came to that. Charly's condition worsened quickly. Before long, he couldn't speak anymore.

My son Dave came from New York. He stayed at the condo and drove me to and from the hospital. I don't know how I would have survived without his support.

Charly's children, Doreen, Theresa, Charles, and Robert, came, too. His sons ignored me, but his daughters and I had a good talk. They told me that their mother and father didn't have a good marriage—they ended up sleeping in separate beds. It had not been a happy home for them or him, and they were pleased that my relationship with Charly was so much better. I didn't want them to feel bad, so I didn't let on what had been happening between us over the past few years.

Although Charly's situation was dire, the doctors had no clear idea of what would happen. They were hoping to find a heart for him in time.

With the future uncertain, his children who had work and other commitments up north, decided to go back to New York. As I drove to my place with Charly's daughters for the last time, we decided to pick up milk at the supermarket, but all the shelves were still empty after Hurricane Andrew. Later that afternoon, they headed to the airport and flew back up north.

The following day, a week after Charly had entered the hospital, Dave and I came home after lunch to freshen up. As I was taking a shower, the phone rang. My heart sank. I had a feeling that it would be bad news, and it was. Charly had died an hour after we left.

It was September 3, the same day my brother Horst passed away in Germany. My mother called me with the news soon after she found out from my sister-in-law. I had hardly slept during the week, and this was just another turn of the screw. It felt like I was living in a bad dream. Little did I know that the nightmare wasn't over yet.

The next morning, I called Charly's daughter Doreen in New York and told her what had happened. After a long silence, she asked, "Where are you going to bury him?"

I said, "I'd like to send him up north and have him buried next to your mother. That's where he belongs."

She said, "Oh, Wally. That is so nice that you'd do that. He told me once that it was too hot in Florida."

So, I flew to New York with the casket. When I got there, Dave, who had preceded me, and Shirley picked me up at Kennedy Airport and took care of everything. When I talked with Charly's children, I asked them to let me know which funeral director he had used for their mother so that I could do the same.

I picked out a casket I thought was appropriate and nice looking. Then, we met with the funeral director—Charly's four children, Dave and I—to discuss how to proceed. I wanted Charly's children to have some input into their father's funeral. They wanted to have two services—one at the Catholic church and another at the burial ground. That made sense to me and I said, "Yes, we'll do that."

I suggested that they—his sons, sons-in-law, grandson, and my son —would be the pallbearers. But Charly's sons said they wouldn't touch their father's casket. They never explained why, and I accepted that, even if it meant hiring six pallbearers.

I ended up paying for everything. After the service at the Catholic church, when the people expressing their condolences had left for the cemetery, the priest came over to us, expecting his fee. Charly's sons just stood there with their hands in their pockets. So, Dave gave him some money. I still don't know what was the matter with them. Perhaps they had no idea what to do when someone dies. I was fortunate that Dave and Shirley were there to support me.

When it was finally over and we said our good-byes, I felt mostly relieved. Perhaps I sound cold a callous, but by the time Charly died, our marriage was on the rocks, and I was angry still about how he had treated me.

By the time I returned to Florida, some of our friends had come back from up north. Edith was especially helpful

At some point, I got a call from Charles. He wanted his father's things, all of them—pictures, passport, jewelry, golf clubs, and clothes. I didn't know how to respond appropriately and called Mrs. Newmark, the attorney who had helped me sell my house in East Northport and done all the paperwork for the closing. She advised me to itemize whatever I was willing to send him and provide her with a copy so she could get money back for what I spent.

Because Charly died without a will, his children contested everything. Mrs. Newmark explained to me that as his wife, I was entitled to half of his estate. They fought me tooth and nail, claiming that I had come into the marriage poor as a church mouse, with nothing of my own. So why should get anything?

They also wanted me to sell the condo and pay them half of the proceeds, and give them the Cougar Charly and I had purchased in March of that year. According to them, they'd never seen me drive it, so as far as they were concerned, it wasn't my car and didn't belong to me.

Mrs. Newmark said, "Don't worry, Wally. I'll take care of you." And she did. I got what was coming to me and kept the condo and the Cougar. I loved that car, and it was my baby for quite some time.

I understand that a lot of people do all kinds of strange things after their parents die. When they are gone, unresolved feelings like anger and disappointment rise to the surface, along with the pain of losing them. If the survivors haven't dealt with their feeling and aren't in good shape themselves, they often act out in ugly and destructive ways. But the way Charly's children tried to take advantage of me was shameful and beyond the pale.

I was married to the man for seven years and did the best I could to be a good wife. Toward the end, things between us became distant and not always pleasant. The aftermath with his children left me feeling with a bad taste for Charly's family. I didn't want anything from them. I didn't want anything to do with them. I didn't even want his name anymore.

When I told Vera how I felt, she said she would talk to her grandson Michael who was an attorney in Pittsburgh. He could take care of it. When he called me, I told him, "I want my first married name back."

He said, "Sure, Wally. No problem. I'll do everything at my end, and you ask your lawyer what you need to do."

Mrs. Newmark told me to get my birth certificate and citizenship papers and fly to Pittsburgh, which is what I did.

Michael picked me up at the airport. He was a young attorney, not long out of law school, but I could tell he was sharp. He took me to his office and had me sign several forms. I paid him and we had dinner together. The next day I flew back to my home in Florida.

A few weeks later, I received a letter from a court in Pittsburgh and an official document that verified my change of name. Reading it, I felt a burden lift from my shoulders. I was a free woman and could be proud of my name again: Wally Stanton.

16

David

After Charly died, I lived alone for some time, but I didn't mind. I had a lot of good friends and enjoyed socializing with them. I started to clean houses and apartments again to help pay for groceries and the condo association fees. I did it for Vera and Sam and cooked for them when Vera became ill. Sam always said, "Wally, you're not a friend, you're family." It was a sad day when Vera died. Sam was inconsolable. After the funeral, his daughter moved him to Pittsburgh, where she could care for him.

In the summer of 1996, when all my friends had gone up north, I developed food poisoning. I had treated myself to my favorite food—raspberries. There was a two-for-one special at the grocery store, and I got two small baskets and ate them all at one sitting. When I started to feel ill that night, I figured I had overdone it. But then I got worse and it became clear that I'd developed food poisoning because the raspberries were contaminated. I was sick in bed for several days and didn't leave my apartment.

When I started to recover and went downstairs to get the mail, I still felt weak. On my way back up, I had to stop from time to time to catch my breath. At some point, someone walked up behind me and said, "Hi. You must be Wally."

I said, "Who are you?"

He introduced himself, "I'm David Cole. I live next door to you."

I suddenly remembered. The apartment owners had decided to rent out their apartment. The woman from the condo association who interviewed David had mentioned it to me. She must have told him my name.

I said, "Nice to meet you." But I was swaying a bit, grabbing on to the banister.

He asked, "What's wrong?" When I told him, he said, "Hold on a minute. I'm going to the store, and I'm going to bring you something." And he left.

I made it back to my place and rested in the living room. Suddenly, there was a knock on the door. When I opened it, there was David, holding out a bottle of Jägermeister, a German liquor made with herbs and spices. I invited him in, and we sat down and talked and drank the dark, anise-flavored liquid. To my surprise, it settled my stomach. The more I drank, the better I felt.

David told me that he'd originally come from Maine but had lived for some time on the Gulf Coast of Florida in a house he shared with one of his sons and his girlfriend. After she and Danny broke up, David moved out, too. He was working for Roadway at the time, a large trucking outfit. When a job opened up at the Fort Lauderdale branch of the company, he decided to take it.

David had been twice divorced and had three sons. The oldest worked for GNC vitamin stores. The middle one, Danny, was not sure what he wanted to do with his life. The youngest had graduated from high school and had gotten into trouble early on. He was a father already, and David's first wife was taking care of the baby.

I liked David right away. He was good-looking and had an carefree manner. It was easy to talk to him, and I told him about my German background, my children, and having been widowed twice.

When it was time for him to leave—he was working at night—he said, "Keep the bottle and use it whenever you're feeling queasy."

I said, "Hold on," and searched for my key to his apartment. The owners had given me a spare in case something broke and needed fixing. I'd look in on the place every now and then to make sure everything was all right, but now I wouldn't have to anymore.

We didn't get a chance to get to know each other better because in August, I went to Germany for four weeks to visit my mother and my cousins. Besides my children, they were the most important people in my life. Berlin was coming into its own after the German government moved its seat there from Bonn. Construction cranes hovered above all parts of the city, and there was building going on everywhere. I hardly recognized my old haunts.

I had a good time with everyone and flew home with no worries, looking forward to meet up with my snowbird friends who were coming back from their summer homes up north.

But shortly after I returned, in September, Brigitte called and said, "Your mother is in bad shape. You better come right away." She was showing signs of dementia and claimed she saw imaginary people standing at the foot of her bed.

I was stunned. During my visit, she had been fine. I made arrangements and arrived in Berlin on a Sunday. My mother was in the hospital and very weak. She looked small and pale. But she recognized me right away and broke into a smile and squeezed my hand when I took hers. By then, she couldn't talk anymore. It was distressing to see her so helpless, but I was happy that I'd made it in time and that she knew her Trauty was with her.

The doctors told us that she didn't have much longer to live. We stayed with her. I stroked her face and told her how much I loved her until she went to sleep and died peacefully early Monday morning.

Brigitte and Dieter made all the funeral arrangements. My mother wanted to be cremated and buried next to my father. I had gone to his grave site during my previous visits to Germany. With space at a premium in Berlin, the cemetery had put up a large stone memorial where people put flowers. A path led to a spot where the ashes were interred in small plots and covered with a marble marker. There was a tall Linden tree to the right whose leaves rustled gently in the wind. It was a quiet, peaceful spot, a good resting place for two people who had experienced so much turmoil and strife in their lives.

I have never gone back to their gravesite, even on subsequent visits to Germany, but I know where it is and have the image in my mind whenever I think of my parents.

I returned to my condo in Margate exhausted, not sure what to do with myself. I felt like an orphan. My children called often to make sure I was all right and told me to pamper myself. My friends helped me grieve.

Over the next few months, David and I got to know each other better. We socialized with people at the clubhouse. All my friends liked him. We went to the beach, attended concerts, and ate out at different restaurants.

When he came home from work in the morning, I'd be sitting in my kitchen having coffee. He would knock on my window and I'd say, "Come on in," and make him breakfast. Then, he'd go to his place to sleep. In the late afternoon, I would knock on the wall between our condos and call out, "I'm cooking meatloaf. You want to come and share it with me?" And we'd have dinner together.

It was easy and relaxing to be with him. I could be myself and didn't have to put on pretenses to meet his expectations, the way I had with Charly. I liked that. David was fun-loving, too. When we went to the laundry room downstairs together to wash our clothes, he'd horse around, hanging my bra and panties on the pole of the carts where dresses and shirts usually went. I'd pretend to be shocked and say, "David, you can't do that. What if someone comes in?"

And he'd grin and say, "So? Let them!"

David was fifty-five, seven years younger than me. At the time, he was younger in spirit, too. He was like a breath of fresh air, clearing away a lot of the cobwebs and unhappy feelings that had accumulated from my time with Charly.

Nine months later, in late spring, he said he was going home to Maine, where his parents, sister and brother lived. His grandfather had started a trucking business in Portland, delivering potatoes. During a country-wide famine when the potato crops failed in all states except Maine, he expanded delivery routes to other states. In time, the company owned restaurants at truck stops as well and had more than 100 employees. David's father and four brothers ran the business until they sold it for a lot of money.

I got the sense that David had a love-hate relationship with his family. He'd left home when he was seventeen, moved into an apartment of his own and gotten a job. He didn't want to work in the family business. Having been on his own for so long, I didn't understand why he would want to move back there.

His son Danny came to help him pack up. By then, David and I had grown close. I missed him when he took off.

A week later, I got a phone call from him. Would I like to come to Maine and meet his parents? "I told them all about you and they want to meet you," he said. "They always went to Germany to buy Mercedes for their salespeople. They like Germans."

"Where would I be staying?" I asked.

"My parents have a big house with extra bedrooms upstairs. Or you can also stay at their cottage on Lake Sebago."

It sounded like a fun adventure. So, I said yes, bought a plane ticket and flew to Portland, Maine. David picked me up at the airport and drove me to his parents' home in one of the suburbs. It was bigger than I expected. I knew his family had money, but I had no idea that they were rich.

David and me at his parent's home.

Everyone was warm and outgoing, except for David's mother. Although Edwina acted friendly toward me, she was often tight-lipped. She had decorated her house from top to bottom when she first married and insisted that it be kept that way. Fifty years later, it looked old-fashioned and a bit shabby. She had grown up in a girl's boarding school after her parents divorced and her father abandoned her family., and wanted things her way. Anything being out of place bothered her.

David's father, Jerry, on the other hand, was a lovely man in his eighties—tall, outgoing, welcoming, and generous. Every Christmas, he gave David and his siblings $20,000 each. I found out later that he had presented Edwina with a million-dollar check for their fiftieth wedding anniversary. She made it clear that she would leave none of the money to her children. Everything would go to the girls' boarding school she had attended. It didn't matter to them because they all knew their father would take care of them.

Conversations around the dinner table were often awkward and strained. It didn't feel like a real family to me. It certainly didn't feel like it to David. I could understand why he'd left home as a teenager and spent as much time away as he could.

Still, his sister Sandy was very nice, and I liked her right away. She was the oldest in the family, about the same age as me, but gray-haired and more on the heavy side. She had two grown daughters and was divorced. She had been working in the local tax collector's office, when she met a former high school classmate who had asked her to a dance more than forty years earlier. They had dated a few times but lost touch following graduation. When he visited his parents in Portland, they reunited. He was getting a divorce himself and wanted to spend time with her.

I didn't meet David's brother Kevin at the time. He was twelve years younger and a lawyer in the military. He had spent time in Vietnam and was currently stationed in Germany, two years away from retirement. I got to know him later on when he returned to the United States.

One day, David took me to Bangor to the Cole Land Transportation Museum that had been created by his uncle Galen. It was a large, gray, one-story building, like a big warehouse. Inside were all kinds of delivery trucks, wagons, fire engines, snowplows, trains, and military vehicles, some of them more than 100 years old; and the entire, original railroad station from Enfield, Maine.

There was a little pamphlet on sale in the gift shop about the founder of the Cole family, and I realized how important the Coles were in Maine's history.

In the meantime, David and Sandy were talking about buying a large motorhome together and traveling all over the United States. It sounded like a lot of fun, and I wished them luck.

I stayed for about a week and had a great time. David and I parted warmly and I went back to Margate, not expecting to see him for a while. I did get postcards from him, marking his progress as he and Sandy traveled out West.

About a month later, I received a call from him. He was in San Diego and had big news. His sister and her high school beau had decided to get together again. She was waiting for him to pick her up and take her to his house in Portland, Oregon. They planned to get married as son as possible.

More significantly, David had been feeling under the weather—fatigued and weak—and when he went to see a doctor, he discovered that he had myelodysplasia, a kind of cancer that affected the blood cells as they formed in his bone marrow. The upshot was that he would have to have monthly examinations.

"But I still want to travel, and I want to travel with you," he said. "Would you like to do that? Would you come to California so we could talk about it further?"

I said, "Yes."

David arranged for a ticket and picked me up at the San Diego airport. At the campground, I met Sandy's boyfriend, who was very nice. We all talked by a campfire, getting to know each other. When Sandy and her beau said good night and left for the motel where they were staying, David and I remained outside sitting at the picnic table and talked.

He explained that he could travel but would have to give himself injections and take a monthly bone marrow test. His doctor in Maine would send his records to whatever hospital he visited, so he could keep going. "I have a lot of feelings for you. I have fallen in love again, and I'm not going to ask you how you feel about me. I know that already. You show it in every way," he said. "I would like you to travel with me and for us to live together."

I started to cry because I felt bad that he'd gotten sick. A lot of thoughts swirled in my head: What would it be like to travel with someone who had a serious illness? Would I know what to do if he got worse? And he was right about how I felt about him, so I didn't hesitate long before saying, "I have feelings for you, too, and I'll go with you, so long as you're being treated."

He said, "If you like, we can drive to your place in Margate and pick up what you need."

And that is what we did. Along the way, I called Shirley and Dave and told them, "I have met somebody who is very nice. I've met his parents, and he asked me to travel with him in a motorcoach, and I want to do that."

Shirley's comment was, "Knowing you, you have already made up your mind."

I said, "Yes, I'm doing it."

Saying it out loud to them cemented my resolve and made it easy for me to commit myself. I was ready for another adventure.

The motorcoach was thirty-three feet long and only two years old. It didn't have a scratch on it. The outside was white and green and had "Tropical" written on the sides next to the image of a palm tree. Inside, it had a big bedroom with a king-size bed, a bath, two closets, and a little nook with a sink to freshen up. The kitchen was part of the living room with a stove, countertop, and microwave across from a table with two benches that folded down to make another bed. At the front of the coach were two comfortable seats for the driver and passenger.

We picked up my belongings in Margate and also bought a trailer that we hooked on the back. That way we could bring my Cougar with us to take day trips and explore.

Our motorhome and my Cougar.

David and I traveled for three years and saw every state in the continental U.S. except for Oklahoma, Nebraska, and Kentucky.

We stayed in Maine for the summer, then took off for Florida, headed west to Texas, and from there drove to California to take the coastal highway north. We visited Sandy and her husband in Portland, Oregon. Their home was located on one of the coastal mountains, right across the street from the Pacific Ocean. It was a beautiful place, but it rained there all the time! They also had a home on the west coast of Florida, and we visited them there, too. The weather was better there!

From Seattle, we headed back east to spend the winter in Florida in my condo in Margate.

During the summers in Maine, we stayed at Sebago Lake, near Portland, where David's parents had a beautiful cabin. David constructed an extension for our motorcoach as well as an outdoor bathroom—he was good with his hands, like Owen. He had built a house in Maine once on his own and often said he would have liked to meet Owen. I created a big flower garden by the side of the motorhome, and David put in steps using old railroad ties. It was quite beautiful. Shirley, Tony, and my two grandchildren came to see us there twice.

Sometimes we drove into town and had dinner with David's parents, or they came to the cottage in Jerry's SUV Mercedes. I cooked dinner for all of us, and we sat outside at the picnic tables and ate. It was a leisurely, relaxed life for everyone.

Edwina and Jerry at the lake.

Even Edwina showed signs of mellowing. She had her own car, a canary yellow Mercedes SUV. One afternoon, she left it in the driveway rather than parking it in the garage, and a powerful storm passed over. The pellets of hail that came down were the size of snowballs and made indentations all over the roof and hood. After that, although she had it fixed, Edwina always called her Mercedes "Dimples."

Jerry and I had a great relationship. I liked his burgundy Mercedes and couldn't help but covet it a little. Since Jerry didn't keep it spotless, I asked him once if I could clean it. He looked at me and gave me the go-ahead. So, I washed and polished until it was spick and span inside and out. When I handed the keys back to him, I said, grinning, "I think that's the closest I've ever been to a Mercedes." He gave me an appraising glance and thanked me.

When the weather started to get cold, we'd take off across America again. David had a KOA guide with all the campgrounds in the United States that could accommodate motorcoaches. In the afternoon, he would tell me where we were and say, "Find us a place where you want to spend the night."

Sometimes, by the time I determined a good location, we'd passed it. But David refused to turn around. He never wanted to backtrack and said, "We'll find another place."

That didn't always work out so well. One night in North Dakota, when we couldn't find a campground, we drove our motorcoach into the woods. It was in the middle of nowhere and spooky and desolate.

I said, "I don't want to be here. If someone comes to make trouble, there is no one to help us."

David said, "There is nothing to worry about. I have a gun and will shoot them." I remained a bit dubious, but his confidence assured me that we'd be all right no matter what happened.

When we got to a campground, we'd park and hook up the toilets, water, and electricity. In the morning, I'd make coffee and breakfast. Then we'd take off and stop by a lake and river for lunch.

The motorhome had everything we needed except a washer and dryer. We would stop in towns along the way to find a laundromat and go grocery shopping.

Sometimes, we'd stay in one place for several days and took my Cougar to explore the area. We saw some of America's great natural wonders—the Grand Canyon, Zion National Park, the Great Salt Lake in Utah, Yellowstone, Mount Rushmore, the Carlsbad Caverns,

Joshua Tree National Park, the Coastal Highway of California, Yosemite, and more. What a beautiful country we have! I have never understood why people want to travel elsewhere when they haven't seen any of the wonderful places in their own nation. I had a good reason to go back to Germany and Berlin from time to time, but I am glad I had the opportunity to discover America, too.

The people we met along the way were great. We'd drive into a campground, and everybody welcomed us. Most campers have given up everything else they owned and spend their life on the road like nomads, meeting up with like-minded travelers. I admired them for their courage and generosity.

At night, they'd build a fire, and everybody would bring something to eat and drink. We sat around and shared stories. No one bragged about "my son is a doctor or lawyer" the way I heard some people do in Florida retirement communities.

One time, near Chicago, we had a big shindig with fifty motorhomes. The next morning at breakfast, one of the campers brought out a big jar filled with jelly beans and we had a raffle. The person who came closest to guessing the right number would get a big plant of violets. Wouldn't you know it? I won!

It was two days after Thanksgiving, and some people had portable fryers in which they cooked turkeys and invited everyone to share their meal. "You can bring the jelly beans," they said with a smile.

We had a feast, and everyone had a good time.

David and I were in our element. He would walk up to anyone and start a conversation. I am like that, too, but with my second husband, I couldn't say boo to our neighbors without him criticizing me for it. David gave me back my sense of self. He appreciated me for who I was. He didn't want me be anyone else. He was even-tempered and never got hot under the collar, not even a little bit. We never argued, we just enjoyed ourselves. Except for my marriage with Owen, being with him was the best time of my life.

David and me on the road.

17

Final Days

Every month of our American journeys, we stopped at a hospital, usually in a large city, so David could get himself checked out. The procedure required drilling into bone and inserting a needle to draw a marrow sample. It was excruciating, but he endured these visits with stoic determination. Holding his hand, I knew how much self-control it required.

David did a lot of reading about his disease. Although there was no agreed-upon cause for myelodysplasia, he often wondered if it didn't run in the family. His younger sister, Rebecca, had developed leukemia at age four. There were no effective treatments for it at the time, and she died two years later. Still, David couldn't be sure what had brought on the disease in his case.

For the most part, he showed no symptoms in the first two-and-a-half years we traveled together. Since we drove at a leisurely pace, with no reason to rush, there were plenty of opportunities for David to take naps and rest up when he felt fatigued.

He did have a lot of night sweats and dreams that caused him to toss and turn. I often took the couch in our living room area to get a good night's sleep.

The nicest hospital we went to was the Virginia Mason Hospital in Seattle. Although David and I weren't married, the staff treated me like his wife. They taught me what I needed to do, including how to give injections, and explained what was in store for me in case the disease progressed and became leukemia.

The last time we were there, the bone marrow test showed just that. Because the medicine injections were no longer as effective as before, the doctors recommended a bone marrow transplant. David's sister and brother had themselves tested and were excellent candidates as donors. David would still be able to travel, but we would have to stay on regular, paved streets and highways and avoid dirt roads because the dust would be a detriment to his health. We knew from experience how difficult it would be to find campgrounds that met those conditions.

I would have to learn to siphon mucus out when it built up in his lungs. I would have to cook differently, too. The doctors recommended a lot of seaweed for David's diet, so I started to make soups with it. Even with creative spicing, neither of us ever grew fond of the taste, but we treated it like medicine and gulped it down. Because David also developed diabetes, I had to measure and weigh his food portions to minimize stress on his digestive system.

For the transplant and recovery period, we would have to live in an apartment no more than fifteen minutes away from the hospital. When I called David's father and explained the situation to him, he said, "Wally, you find what you need, and I'll take care of the money. Don't worry about it." His generosity took a load off my shoulders. He was already paying for David's pharmaceuticals, which were quite expensive.

With all that, the doctors predicted that a bone marrow transplant would have only a 50-50 chance of success and that, in all likelihood, David would not live more than five years.

As I drove him from that consultation to our motorhome in my Cougar, David said, "You know, I don't know if I want to do it. They can't guarantee the results. They can't tell me how much longer I'll live. They don't know." He turned to me. "What do you think I should do?"

I said, "I can't tell you that. But I want you to know, whatever you decide, I'll be right here. Whatever needs to be done, I'll do it for you to the best of my ability. I'll go to the end of the world with you."

He stared straight ahead, thinking. Then, he said, "You know what? I'm not going to do it. Let's get back to the camper and take off. Life is pretty good right now. Let's enjoy it while we can."

I nodded in agreement.

We drove in silence for a while until Dave spoke up again, "You know what I'd really like to do? I'd like to go to Germany. You think we can do that?"

I said "I don't see why not."

When I called my cousin Brigitte and her husband, they said, "Of course you can come." We could have their apartment because they always stayed in their cottage during the summer months.

Brigitte and Dieter Larisch.

So, we drove to Maine, got tickets, and flew to Germany. Brigitte and Dieter lived in a small apartment on Torfstrasse in the Moabit

District, west of downtown Berlin. Because their Murphy beds were always down, there was only a narrow gap between them and the cabinets against the wall. But their living room was spacious and comfortable.

We settled in with no difficulty. In the mornings, we'd have a cup of coffee and take the bus to their garden cottage. It was only two stops away, in another part of Moabit.

Dieter had rented a car, and we all piled in for that day's adventure. He acted as our chauffeur and drove us everywhere. By then, he had taken early retirement, and with his pension and income from investments, he was making more money each month than when he worked as a high-level manager for the baking goods company. I was glad that he and Brigitte had such a good life.

I showed David where I'd grown up. Weddingstrasse still had cobblestones, but the apartment building was gone. It had been demolished and replaced by a small corner park with a hedge on three sides and tall needle trees. We sat on one of the benches. It was quiet and serene and you couldn't hear the city traffic at all—a little spot of paradise. I thought of my parents. It was a better place to spend time with them than at their graveside.

We also went to the Badstrasse but the leather goods store was no longer there.

After a week in Berlin, we drove all over Germany. Dieter had grown up in Bavaria and knew his way around back and mountain roads. He showed us castles and country inns I'd never seen before.

In Karlsruhe on the Rhine River, Brigitte and I went to a spa and had mud baths. My mother had always been enthusiastic about them. When she worked for Siemens, the company paid for their employees to vacation in spa towns—they all have *Bad* (bath) as part of their names, like Bad Kreuznacht, Wiesbaden, and the most famous one, Baden Baden.

The men wanted to have nothing to do with it, but Brigitte and I were eager to try it. At first, it felt odd to climb into a bathtub and have the attendants pile on warm, black mud until my body was completely covered, but then I started to enjoy it, although I didn't like it when they put it on my face. It felt so relaxing I wanted to go to sleep. I can't speak to any lingering health benefits, but I would gladly do it again.

Sometimes, it was difficult for Dave to walk, but he soldiered on as best he could. The hardest times were at night. He perspired heavily, and by morning his bed was soaked. I was concerned that it would ruin the feather bed filled with Eider down in the Berlin apartment, but Brigitte said not to worry.

David got along very well with our hosts. His humor, curiosity and positive disposition endeared him to them. Brigitte often said, "David is just like Owen."

At some point, we visited a car dealership. I had mentioned to David that I'd always wanted a Mercedes, and he was ready to buy one. But the Euro had just replaced the German mark, and the salesman was not interested in Americans as customers. Or, perhaps he did not want to go through the rigmarole of shipping the car to the United States. In any case, we left empty-handed.

I felt only a twinge of regret because we'd spent three splendid weeks in Germany. We were sad when our time with Brigitte and Dieter came to an end, but we flew home with a lot of good memories.

After we got back to Portland, David went to the hospital for another test. When they drilled into his bone, it hurt so bad that he started to scream. Afterward, the bandaged wound became infected and he had to spend more time in the hospital to recover. The prognosis was not good. By then, the disease had turned into full-fledged leukemia. The medications he injected no longer worked.

We stayed at the lake for the remainder of the summer and enjoyed watching the leaves turn red and yellow in the crisp fall weather.

One day, David said to me, "I don't feel good. I have to go to the hospital."

As he was getting into the car, he said, "Go and get my papers in the cupboard next to the bedroom. They're my last will and living will. Whatever happens, I don't want them to extend my life unnecessarily."

I said, "I don't need them. I'm going to bring you home after they treat you."

He said, "I don't think I'm going to come back home."

His words struck me like a blow, but I acted like I didn't believe him.

When I had settled David in the hospital, I called his father and told him what was happening. He said, "Wally, come on over."

I drove to his house and told him and Edwina what David had said. Jerry sighed and said, "Well, he's in good hands in the hospital. Do you have his papers?"

"Yes, they're in the motorhome."

"Well, then that's all right."

David's condition changed from day to day, but he improved enough to become hopeful again. He asked the doctors if he could travel, and they said yes. If he started to feel bad, he should go to a hospital for treatment until he recovered.

I was pleased and said, "Okay then, let's travel."

We made plans to winterize the motorhome—I would take care of that—and drive it to Florida, where Christopher, his oldest son, lived. When David was ready, I would fly back to Portland, and we'd take a plane together to Jacksonville. He wanted to check out the hospital there to see if the doctors had other options for treatment than what Seattle and the Mayo Clinic offered.

Danny, David's second oldest son, and his girlfriend had come for a visit, and we took off together in the motorhome. We made it to Orlando on Thanksgiving Day.

When I called David, he sounded okay but said, "You know what, I have developed hemorrhoids, and the doctors want to operate. What do you think?" I said, "If it needs to be done, let them."

But it sounded odd to me, so I called Jerry who said he had heard nothing of the sort from David. He attributed it to him drifting in and out of reality because of his medication. That didn't sound right to me either, so I told him, "I'm coming back."

I called my son, who arranged a ticket for me. By the time I got to Portland and the hospital, the doctors had sedated David to the point that he could no longer speak. He could hear and respond yes by squeezing my hand. But he was hooked up to so many gadgets and drip lines that he looked like a creature in a horror movie. David was a big guy and it nearly broke my heart to see him lying there so helpless and hardly able to move.

David's mother stood next to his bed like a statue and never touched him, never talked to him, but I could tell that she was devastated. His father was very loving, speaking to David, holding his hand.

Jerry was kind enough to let me stay at their house in one of the upstairs bedroom. When we called David's sister Sandy, Jerry told her she needed to come. She said she couldn't because she had no winter clothes. Even after her father mentioned that she could go shopping with me for what she needed and he'd pay for it, she refused.

We called David's three sons to come to see their father. The youngest missed his plane. Dan came with his girlfriend, and Christopher made it, too. By then, such a crowd of David's relatives and friends had assembled that the nurses put up a screen by his door and let in only members of his immediate family.

I sat by his head and stroked his hair. Dave had often mentioned that he wished he could have met Owen. I could always tell him about my first husband, and he listened without displaying an ounce of jealousy. So, I said to him, "You're going to heaven and Owen is waiting for you, and you're going to talk about building houses." I don't know if he heard me. I kept watching his stomach rise and fall as he breathed.

At some point, it stopped and he was gone.

I burst into tears and sat there crying like a helpless child. When I got myself under control, I kissed him good-bye and left the room.

His father put his arm around me and said, "He's in heaven now."

I nodded, "I know."

David's mother said nothing but walked away and stood off to one side by herself, doing everything she could to preserve her dignity.

The funeral took place in Enfield, about 150 miles north-northeast of Portland. David's grandfather had built a cemetery there for family and friends. It was a wooded area and very peaceful. Everyone in David's family except his sister, attended. It was a large gathering. Many of hi uncles and cousins I had never met before introduced themselves to me.

At the reception afterward, I talked to David's childhood friend Clay. I had met him several times during our earlier stays in Portland. He was Jamaican and his wife was a Danish woman named Inga. He told me that he'd often said to David, "Why don't you marry Wally?" and David told him, "I feel like I'm married to her."

To me, David had said once, "You're more than a wife."

He just assumed I was okay with our arrangement. I never told him that I was reluctant to marry him because I had already had two husbands die on me. Now I had lost my third, married or not.

After the funeral services, David's aunt Candy came up to me and said, "Wally, if you want to be buried here, you're welcome to. You can be buried right next to David."

I thanked her and said, "I already have a place by my first husband."

She nodded. "Well, I just wanted to let you know how grateful we are for all the things you did for my nephew."

I realized that if I had married David, I would have been set for life. His family would have taken care of me. But I never thought of that when we were together, and I don't have any regrets about how things turned out. I only wish he and I could have had more time together.

When we returned to Portland, I got another surprise. The next morning after breakfast, David's father tossed a bunch of brochures on the table and said, "Today I'm going to buy you a Mercedes."

I was astonished and couldn't believe my ears. But then he added, "David told me, 'When I am gone, I want you to buy Wally a Mercedes!' and that's what I'm going to do."

At the dealership, there was a gray, two-door SL 350 that had been turned in over the weekend. It had belonged to a realtor, who realized she needed a four-wheel drive in Maine during the winter, and it was less than a year old. Jerry asked me if I liked it. I would have preferred a pale blue model, but I wasn't going to tell him that. I took it for a test drive and it purred and glided along the road like a skater on smooth ice. So, I said yes.

Jerry paid $42,500 for it. Then, he handed me the keys and said, "Now you are even closer than when you washed mine."

I was touched that he'd remembered.

The question remained how to get it to Florida. David had mentioned to his father that he could ship it, but I said, "No, we're going to drive it!"

Jerry was 88 years old, however, and I wasn't going to let him drive that car. Besides, it was too far to make the trip in one day. I suggested that David's oldest son could do it and that Jerry could stay home because it was winter, after all. But he didn't want to hear of it.

So, Jerry and Christopher drove the Mercedes to Florida, and I took a plane. I guess we all wanted to put some distance between us and what we'd been through. When they arrived in Margate two days later, we all went out to dinner together.

The next day, I drove Jerry to the Fort Lauderdale airport. He thanked me again for all I had done for his son and embraced me. Then we said good-bye. I looked after him as he walked into the building. I knew that I would never see him again.

I was amazed that Dave had thought about doing something for me after he would be gone. It was so like him. Giving me a Mercedes was such a thoughtful, generous, loving present. Whenever I got in to drive it, I thought of him and the good times we had together.

I loved my husband Owen most of all, but I loved Dave, too, with all my heart. He was so strong, so determined to live. I am glad that I could be there for him when he needed me. When I think back on it now, I know that we were good for each other. I made him happy, and he kept going as long as he did because of me. His parents were too old to do anything for him directly, so I took care of him. And he gave me back my belief in myself and the courage to go on.

David L. Cole
July 24, 1941 - November 29, 2000

18
Wrapping Up

I had stayed in touch with a number of the people David and I met while traveling across America in our motorhome. Some had lost their spouses too, in the meantime, and asked if I wanted to join them as "co-pilot" for further adventures on the road. I was very touched, but I just couldn't bring myself to do it.

So, I returned to Margate. I was sixty-five years old and, living alone with time on my hands, I questioned myself more than in the past. During the day, I kept busy cleaning apartments, sewing, crocheting, and attending various activities at the clubhouse. But at night before going to bed, the walls started to close in and everything kind of overwhelmed me. I turned on the television or radio because I hated the silence that left me alone with my thoughts.

I kept asking myself: Why I was being punished? What had I done to deserve such a fate? Every husband and good man I met and loved had died on me. Then, some of my girlfriends said to me, "It's because they all knew you could make it by yourself. You're strong enough and you can do everything you decide to do for yourself." It gave me some comfort, but I still felt bereft.

My friends continued to support me. I became especially close to three women, Joan, Shirley, and Rose. It was a coincidence that two of them had the same name as my daughter and daughter-in-law. We called ourselves the four musketeers and were almost inseparable. We participated in a lot of activities at the clubhouse, went to the movies together, gambled at casinos for fun, took shopping trips, and played cards most evenings.

For Christmas I always flew up north to Long Island and stayed with Shirley and Tony or Dave and Rosie. But I always came back to spent New Year's Eve with my friends.

In 2009, I took a trip to Germany in December because I wanted to see Berlin during the holidays. To my delight, my granddaughter Diana joined me between Christmas and New Year's when she had a week off.

We had a great time, going to the Christmas market at the Alexanderplatz in the center of the city. There were lights everywhere, a carousel for children, and a giant Tannenbaum, all decorated and glowing. We had *Glühwein* (literally: glow wine—hot, spiced wine) and *Krapfen* (jelly donuts) dusted with powdered sugar as we wandered among the all the booths selling toys, shiny ornaments, retail items, and all kinds of food.

We had a great reunion with of all of my cousins. I was able to show Diana where I grew up on Weddingstrasse, where I worked, and where I met my husband, her grandfather.

The only sobering experience was our visit to the Peter Fechter memorial, my second time. I was surprised how it had changed since the Wall came down. By then, the Zimmerstrasse was an ordinary shopping street and the cross had been replaced by a simple, copper colored obelisk with the inscription "Peter Fechter, 1944-1962 ... *er wollte nur die Freiheit*—he just wanted freedom." I felt a stab of anguish in my heart thinking back on my wartime experiences.

I had happier memories when we went to the Airlift Memorial and Museum, where a partial concrete arch resembling the beginning of a bridge stood at the edge of a meadow at the northwest corner of Berlin's Tempelhof Airport. I told Diana all about how the heroic efforts of the Candy Bombers of the Americans and their allies saved us from starvation.

Diana and me before the Airlift Memorial.

On New Year's Eve, we joined the crowd at the Brandenburg Gate to celebrated with tens of thousands of people. We were all bundled up because it was so cold we could see our breath, but it was fantastic. Just as in communities across the globe, when the countdown reached zero, we cheered and watched the fireworks to welcome the new year.

That spring, for my 75th birthday, my Margate friends threw me a big party at the clubhouse. There was food, beer, and wine, and dancing.

Five years later, I decided to celebrate my 80th birthday in my apartment. One the eve of March 10, all my friends assembled there for an early dinner. At some point, there was a knock on the door, and a package arrived from my children via special delivery. The attached card said that under no circumstances should I open it before my actual birthday.

My friends all said, "Well, in that case, we'll stay until after midnight. You can open it then."

When the clock struck twelve, I tore the packaging off and opened the box. It contained a faux book whose cover Shirley had decorated with pictures of European castles and beer steins. Inside, was an airplane ticket to Germany and a toiletry travel kit. I was touched. What a wonderful present!

I flew to Berlin, where Brigitte and Dieter picked me up at the airport. To my surprise, that evening Dieter's bowling friends threw me another birthday party in a restaurant whose name was "Paulaner," like the Munich beer. More than thirty people came. Many remembered me from previous visits, and we had a wonderful evening, laughing, trading stories, and drinking beer.

A few days later, we drove to Bavaria to visit my niece, Heike, who lives near the city of Nuremberg. She and her husband held yet another birthday party for me, and many of her neighbors attended. Forewarned, I had asked that no one buy me any presents, although I would be happy accept to birthday cards because they were so pretty in Germany.

Everywhere I went, I had a marvelous time, but there was a melancholy undercurrent, too. Especially when I walked through the areas of Berlin I remembered from when I was girl, and when I spent time in the park on the corner of Weddingstrasse where my parent's apartment building had stood. I realized that I was saying good-bye. It was likely the last time I'd see everyone, and I tried to etch faces and places in my memory. I don't think I will visit Germany again, not unless I have a travel companion.

A year later, I was delighted to attend the wedding of my grand-daughter Diana. She and her husband-to-be, Adrian, had been living in Connecticut for some time.

Diana and Adrian.

The nuptials took place at the West Sayville Country Club, a popular wedding venue on the southern shore of Long Island, and the weekend was filled with lots of activities. Adrian's parents flew in from Ireland. With his large extended family of aunts, uncles, and cousins on both sides of the Atlantic Ocean, and the throng of Diana's many friends, it was a big affair.

For the bridal shower, I was able to partially realize my dream of running a flower shop by making all the floral center pieces on the tables, using carnations and roses. They were a big hit, and people attending took them home.

The ceremony was held on the grounds of the country club under a floral trellis in view of the ocean. Joe, the uncle of Shirley's husband, was a minister and presided over Diana's and Adrian's marriage vows. It was a beautiful event.

Since then, they have settled Ohio, and I am glad that they are building a good life together.

For me, the wedding came with an additional benefit. I met a freelance journalist there who wrote for various newspapers and magazines. She and I got to talking, and when I told her about my past adventures, she decided to write an article about me. Her piece, "Profile of a War Bride," was published in *Senior Times*. I was surprised when it came out and she sent me a copy. Reading it, rekindled my interest in writing this book, which I had wanted to do for some time.

Meanwhile, my Margate friends were all moving into assisted living facilities or passing on, and I was becoming increasingly isolated.

In 2016, Shirley and Tony persuaded me that I should not be living alone anymore. They were moving to the West Coast of Florida and invited me to join them. So, in November of that year, I sold my apartment in Margate and moved to Venice, near Sarasota, to be closer to my daughter and son-in-law. I live in a place of my own, about ten minutes away from them.

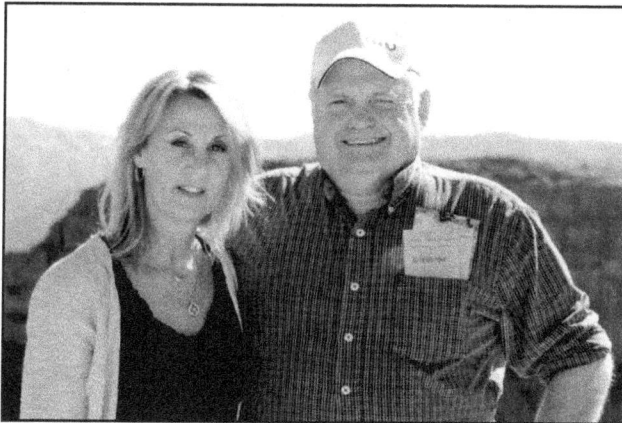

Shirley and Tony.

Much as I hated to let go of it, I gave my Mercedes to Tony. The blistering Florida sun and salty sea air had not been kind to it. But while the paint was fading and peeling in places, the car was in excellent shape. It had no dents and only 38,000 miles on the odometer. Tony drove it to New York and kept it there to use when he visited my grandson, Anthony.

But the weather took its toll on the car there, too.

At some point, Tony returned from one of his trips and said, "Wally, I have good news and bad news. It depends on how you take it. I sold the Mercedes."

I said, "That's good news."

"And I got $400 for it."

"That's good news, too," I said. "What's the bad news?"

We both laughed.

I used the money as a down payment to go on a cruise to St. Martin, St. Thomas and the Bahamas with my daughter and granddaughter—three generations of Stanton women having fun together!

Anthony.

My grandson Anthony and I get along well, too, although that wasn't always the case. When he and Diana were children and visited me in Margate, they slept on the pull-out sofa in the living room. In the mornings, Anthony liked to jump up and down on it. When I told him to stop, he often ignored me, the way young, rambunctious boys do when they're having fun. So, I put my foot down. After I got mad and yelled at him a couple of times, he listened but also decided I didn't like him.

Fortunately, we cleared the air between us a while ago. He comes to Florida a lot to visit his parents and me. He has always been big and now that he is six-foot-four and very strong, he gives me a bear hug and lifts me off the floor to say hello when he arrives.

To say I have a wonderful family would be an understatement. My children, Shirley and Dave, and grandchildren, Diana and Anthony, give me much joy. My son-in-law, Tony, has helped me in so many ways. My son's wife, Rosie, has become like a daughter to me. I love them all dearly.

Dave and Rosie.

I don't believe in staring in the rear view mirror for too long, but when I do glance back, I know I've been blessed.

My parents were loving and encouraged me to follow my dreams. I had a good life with my husband Owen for twenty-nine years. Some people I know never had such an opportunity. I spent three years traveling all over the United States with another man who was generous and kind.

Growing up in Berlin during the Second World War, made me stronger and more self-reliant than many other people I know. I had to fend for myself from early on and continue to take care of myself in whatever ways I can. Perhaps I'm just too stubborn, but I don't give up easily. I don't ever say, "I can't do that."

I watched my father and later on, Owen, fix all kinds of things and learned from them to do the same. People have asked me to hang pictures for them, replace the heads on the showers, hang curtain rods, change toilet seats, and paint furniture. If I don't know how to do it, I'll find out.

I still have the toolbox Owen gave me when we lived on the farm in Coxsackie so I could keep my own set of tools. (I store it outside on the lanai because, after all these years, it still has a faint smell of cow manure. I swear it does!).

Whenever I go to Home Depot, I think of Owen and say, "Oh, hon, if you were alive today, you'd love this place. You'd be here all the time."

Following him to the United States was the best decision I ever made. I love this country that has given me so much, and I deeply appreciate the freedom and opportunities it provides to everyone. You can work hard and make something of yourself here. I would not want to live anywhere else in the world. I am proud to be an American.

For myself, I continue to enjoy visits from my children and grand-children and socializing with my friends and neighbors.

From left: Anthony, Shirley and Tony, me, Diana, Rosie and David.

Now that I am in my mid-eighties, I have slowed down a bit, but I keep busy taking care of my home, crocheting, and puttering about my garden.

I continue to be curious about the world and love to talk to all kinds of people.

I am not afraid of having new experiences and adventures. I look forward to them

I want to make many more new friends.

And I plan to be around for a good while longer.

www.ingramcontent.com/pod-product-compliance
Lightning Source LLC
Chambersburg PA
CBHW031131090426
42738CB00008B/1042